Wild Blooms & Colorful Creatures

15 Appliqué Projects • Quilts, Bags, Pillows & More

by Wendy Williams

Publisher: Amy Marson

Creative Director: Gailen Runge

Art Director / Cover Designer: Kristy Zacharias

Editor: Lynn Koolish

Technical Editors: Susan Nelsen and Alison M. Schmidt

Book Designer: Katie McIntosh

Production Coordinator: Jenny Davis

Production Editor: Katie Van Amburg

Illustrator: Tim Manibusan

Photography by John Doughty | Spy Photography, unless otherwise noted

Published by C&T Publishing, Inc., P.O. Box 1456, Lafayette, CA 94549

Library of Congress Cataloging-in-Publication Data

Williams, Wendy, 1961-

Wild blooms & colorful creatures : 15 appliqué projects : quilts, bags, pillows & more / by Wendy Williams.

pages cm

ISBN 978-1-60705-872-4 (soft cover)

1. Quilting--Patterns. 2. Appliqué--Patterns. I. Title. II. Title: Wild blooms and colorful creatures.

TT835.W53495 2014

746.46--dc23

2013023073

Printed in China

Dedication

I dedicate this book to my mum and dad, who were amazing parents and were always proud of my accomplishments.

Acknowledgments

I would like to thank:

My family, for their patience and support—especially my husband, George, who, among other things, cooks for me every night while I carry on working; my children, Taylor and Isaac, who happily throw in comments when I ask for their opinion on my designs; my sisters, Annette and Gwennyth, who introduced me to quilting and are always proud of what I do; my brother Garry, who runs my website; and Jenn, who always kindly offers advice and opinions when asked.

My many friends with whom I have far too little time to be with—especially Narelle, who encouraged me to start my business, and Nola, who always listens.

Kathy Doughty, who has given so much. I have no doubt that I wouldn't be where I am without her support, inspiration, and encouragement.

The talented staff at Material Obsession, who make my life fun and who inspire me every day.

John Doughty, who did the photography. I had total faith that he would make my quilts look amazing.

All the students who take my classes. I do this for them—they inspire me and make what I do worthwhile.

Everyone who makes my quilts and buys my patterns—without them, I couldn't carry on doing this as my "job."

Contents

Introduction

The projects in this book combine a variety of fabrics, including cotton solids and prints, linen, and wool. By combining different patterns and textures, and with a touch of fun and imagination added in, you can achieve stunning, contemporary projects. You can't help but have fun, because the techniques are simple and easy to achieve for all lovers of stitching. Working with color is always cheery and good for the soul. You can even add extra embellishment to the designs with buttons and beads—the only limit is your imagination.

The projects include flowers, birds, houses, and animals. You can mix up the designs from project to project and make some unique items of your own. Wool felt is a great way to gain confidence with color, because you can make up all of the design elements and then audition them onto different backgrounds. Keep playing until you find the one that makes your heart sing.

Getting Started

Combining Wool and Cotton

We are all used to working with traditional cotton fabrics for our quilts. Combining linen and wool with cotton adds a new dimension. Use fabrics with designs such as flowers, circles, leaves, and paisleys for flower centers, birds, butterflies, and dragonflies. The prints add interest, light, and shade, as well as a little more punch, especially when they are fussy cut.

After working on a few of these projects, you will start to look at fabrics with a different eye. The simple shapes for the appliqué are easy to cut and stitch, and one project tends to lead to another. Soon you will end up with a variety of completed masterpieces. This is a time to throw caution to the wind and try something new where there are few rules.

Appliqué Basics

Wool

Wool is available in a great range of textures and blends. I like pure wool, but wool blends can be used as well. Try to choose wools that are either felted or have a tight weave. Wool fabrics with a looser texture can be backed with fusible (iron-on) interfacing to give them more stability and to reduce the fraying on the edges. I use wool on projects that do not require a lot of durability, such as a wallhanging.

Wool also comes in a variety of colors and textures. Heavily textured wool that has a fuzzy or furry texture is great to use for animals.

Before you begin, there are a few things to consider in order to get the best outcome from wool:

- Before using wool fabric, check for colorfastness by wetting the wool and steam pressing it on top of a piece of white cotton fabric. If there is no color bleed, then it is fine to use. If the color bleeds, you need to prewash the wool separately using a color catcher to catch any excess dye and to see whether the color has run.
- Wool should also be preshrunk prior to cutting. You can do this by washing it or by giving it a good steam press.
- Wool that is not machine washable can often be felted. To do this, prepare the wool in a washing machine with hot water and detergent. Dry it in the clothes dryer on hot to complete the felting process. Then give the wool a good steam press. Wool that is machine washable cannot be felted.
- Thrift shops are often a good source of wool. You can buy used wool clothes and blankets and cut them into usable pieces.
- You can also experiment with dyeing wool. If you throw fabrics with different colors and textures into the same dye bath, you will get an array of different shades of one color.

Wool Felt

Wool felt is my preferred medium. It is more durable than wool, which means it can be used on items that will receive a fair amount of use, such as a bag or pillow. It has a very soft feel and is a pleasure to work with. You should use only pure wool felt; synthetic craft felt is not suitable, as it will pill and wear over time.

- Wool felt tends to shrink, so either prewash it in cold water or steam press it. Check for colorfastness as you did for wool fabric (see page 5). I don't prewash mine, but I do give it a good steam press. The wool felt that I use is machine washable and colorfast.
- Wool felt is a delight to work with because the edges are so clean once they are cut. You can let your imagination run wild—cut shapes as simple or as intricate as you like. Small circles that are quite tricky in other forms of appliqué are easy in wool felt.
- When stitching the wool felt, you need only take a small stitch into the fabric, as the edges won't fray.
- When cutting wool felt, make sure that you get a neat, smooth edge, as this will be the finished edge.
- Wool felt gives a lovely soft effect and stands out beautifully on heavily quilted backgrounds.
- Wool felt comes in an array of colors, from bright to soft pastels. It has a very soft feel and is a pleasure to work with.

Choosing Threads for Appliqué

When selecting threads, anything goes. You can use a variety of threads to attach wool to the background and to make embellishments. I like to use size 5 and 8 perle cottons, as they are readily available. You can use any embroidery threads, including stranded embroidery thread, which allows you to choose the number of strands depending on how fine or thick you want the stitching to be. Whichever thread you choose, you will need a variety of colors. As you work with this appliqué technique, you can slowly build up a wide color palette. The projects in this book are also great for using all those fancy threads that you may have in your collection. Try some metallic and variegated threads. You really can't make a mistake.

For my style of appliqué, I like all of the stitching to be a feature. Therefore, I tend not to use the wool threads that are usually associated with wool appliqué. If you use these threads, keep in mind that they blend in beautifully with wool. If you want your stitching to stand out, you can add embellishing threads later.

Using Freezer Paper for Appliqué

I use freezer paper to make my appliqué templates. It's easy, convenient, and works for needle-turn and raw-edge appliqué.

1. Trace the appliqué patterns onto the dull (paper) side of the freezer paper and cut on the drawn lines.

2. Use an iron to press the freezer-paper templates onto the right side of the appropriate wool, wool felt, cotton, or linen fabric. The shiny side of freezer paper is plastic and sticks to fabric. You can peel the templates right off when you are done and use them several times before they won't stick anymore.

3. Cut the appliqué pieces:

- For woven fabrics, such as cotton or linen, trace around the freezer paper and cut each piece with a ¼″ seam allowance, then see the technique in Needle-Turn Appliqué (page 7).
- For wool or wool felt, cut along the edge of the template for raw-edge appliqué. There is no need to trace around the template or to leave a seam allowance.

4. Remove the freezer-paper template.

Needle-Turn Appliqué

For my style of needle-turn appliqué, just turn under the fabric on the drawn line after tracing and cutting the appliqué pieces. Use a running stitch (page 9) to stitch close to the turned edge. On corners and inward curves, it may be necessary to make a small stitch over the edge to hold the fabric securely.

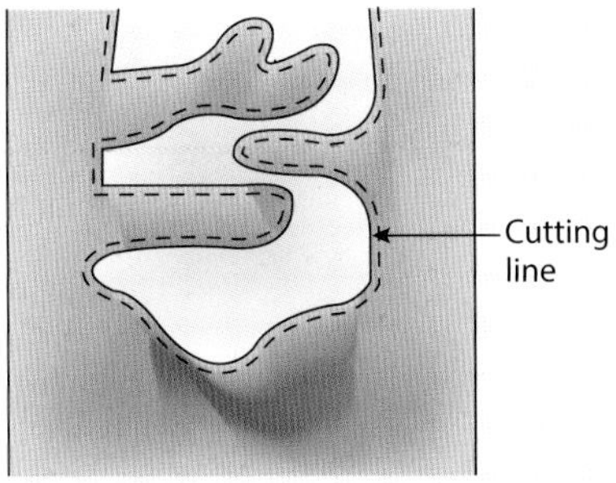

Cut just outside drawn line.

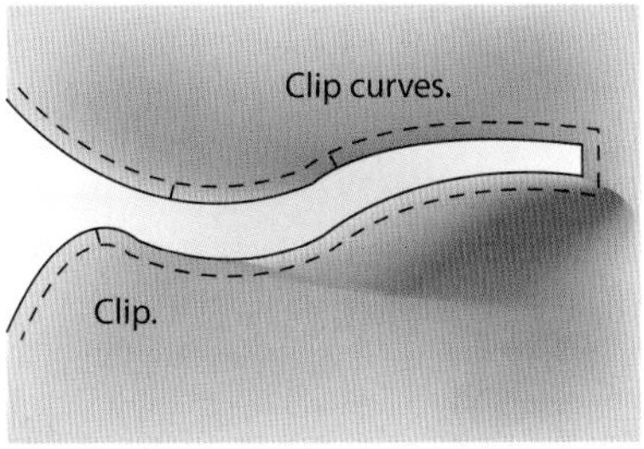

Clip curves as needed.

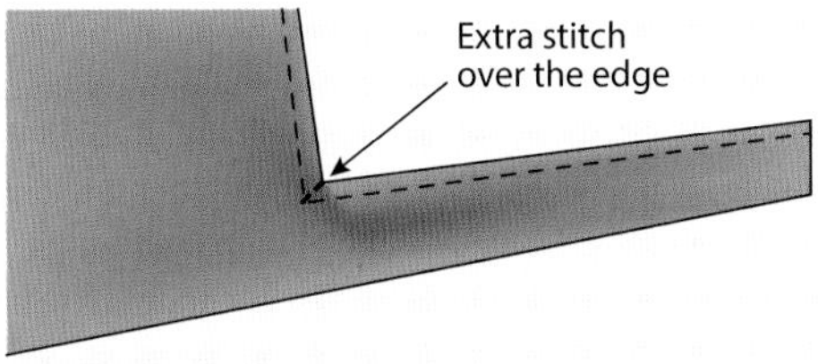

Use extra stitch in inward corners.

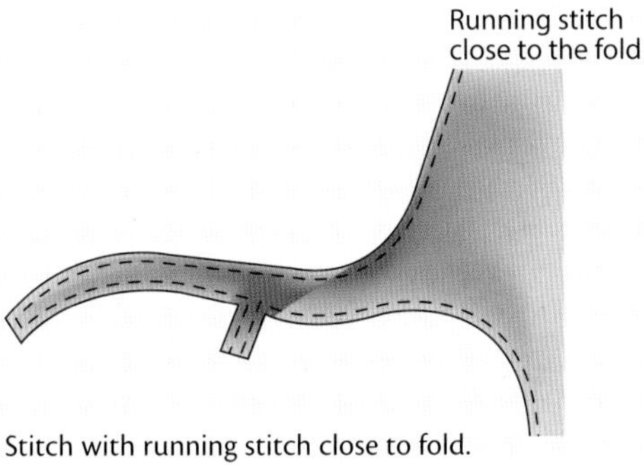

Stitch with running stitch close to fold.

Needles for Appliqué

You can use a variety of needles, such as embroidery, straw, and chenille, in a range of sizes. You may already have most of these needles in your sewing kit.

Embroidery needles work well for all the basic stitches. You may want to use chenille needles when working on linen, because they are easy to thread with perle cotton and have a nice sharp point.

Straw needles or milliners needles are great for making colonial knots and French knots. The needle width is an even thickness along its length, including the eye, which makes wrap stitches much easier to do.

That being said—in the end, use any needle that works well for you.

Scissors

I am quite particular about the scissors I use for cutting my wool and wool felt. My favorite pair has a blade length of approximately 2″ (5cm) and a blunt end. They aren't particularly expensive, but they cut beautifully. I can cut most of my shapes with this pair. To cut small circles, I use a smaller blade. To cut large trees and so on, I use my everyday fabric scissors, which have a 5″ (13cm) blade. Remember to keep your scissors exclusively for fabric. Use a cheap, everyday pair of scissors for cutting paper patterns.

Cutting

The appliqué shapes can be cut out freehand, or you may prefer to use freezer-paper templates. When cutting the wool and wool felt, you don't need to add a seam allowance; when the designs overlap, just make sure to leave a small amount to tuck under.

I like to do as much of the decorating as I can before I appliqué the shape to the background. It is much easier to work with the pieces when they are small, and they are much more portable that way. This also gives me the option of auditioning the shapes on different backgrounds. I often have a few background fabrics beside me while I work so that I can place the pieces onto them when they are done and get a feeling for the color combinations. Don't be afraid to change your mind on your background choice as you work; it is all a part of the process.

Using a Design Wall

I always use a design wall or board to audition fabrics for the background and appliqué. You can make a simple board, which is great for smaller projects, by stapling polyester batting over an artist's canvas.

I use flat-head pins or appliqué pins to hold the appliqué pieces in place until they are stitched.

You can use glue baste or gluesticks to hold the shapes in place temporarily instead of pinning. If you do use glue, use it sparingly, as it can make it more difficult to stitch through an area that is glued.

Backgrounds

You can choose wool, cotton, or linen for the background, depending on the look you are trying to achieve.

- Wool looks softer and has more of a folk or country look. You can piece the backgrounds or use the wool as a wholecloth background. If you are piecing the wool for a background, it is better to press the seams open to reduce bulk. Alternately, you may like to press the seams together and topstitch the seam to the background by hand or machine.
- Cotton is great for bed quilts, as it is finer and more readily available. Cotton is also available in a larger range of colors and patterns than wool. Using printed backgrounds tends to give the quilt a more contemporary look. You can piece the background or use the cotton as a wholecloth. If using it as a wholecloth, however, you are restricted to the width of the fabric—it will be approximately 44″ (110cm) wide maximum. You can easily add borders using any of your favorite traditional blocks.
- Linen is beautiful to use as a background, as it is delightful to embroider on. Also, widths up to 58″ (150cm) are available. Linen comes in a wide range of colors, textures, patterns, and prints. Linen/cotton blends are also great to work with. When appliquéing onto linen, you may need to neaten (zigzag or overlock) the outer edges, as linen tends to fray more easily because of its more open weave.

Batting

I use high-loft wool batting in my quilts, as it gives extra dimension to the quilt after it is quilted. I like to machine quilt the background heavily. Outlining the appliqué makes the shapes stand out or pop on a completed quilt. Wool batting also gives quilts a soft, modern feel.

Laundering

Quilts made from a mixture of wool, linen, and cotton are as washable as any other quilt. I have product tested a piece that was appliquéd with many colors of wool on a solid background. I machine washed it by throwing it into the machine with a load of my everyday washing (not something I would normally do with my quilts). Even without pressing, it performed beautifully.

Appliqué patterns for all the projects are at the back of the book, starting on page 73. Some of the larger patterns are on the pullout pages. You'll notice that the appliqué patterns are not numbered, and there is no placement diagram to show you exactly where to place each piece. Instead, you are referred to the project photograph and given free rein to place the appliqués as you choose. While you may closely follow the placements that I have used, you may also decide to strike out on your own and follow your own whims. Either way, enjoy!

Embroidery Stitches

BACKSTITCH

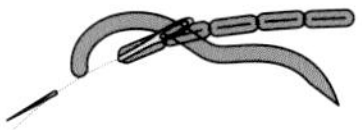

CHAIN STITCH

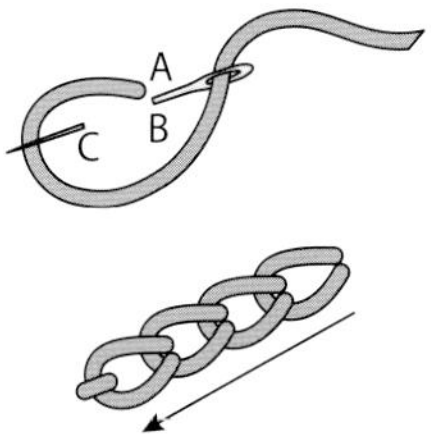

COLONIAL KNOT

CROSS STITCH

FLY STITCH

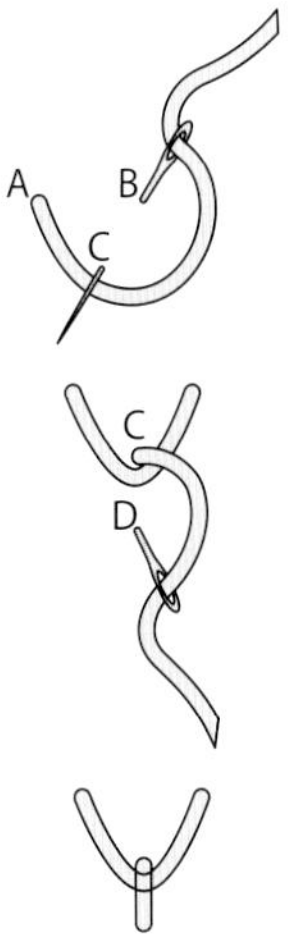

FRENCH KNOT

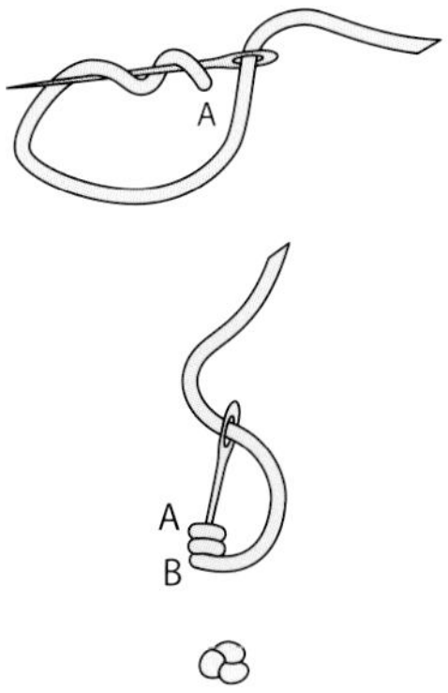

HERRINGBONE STITCH

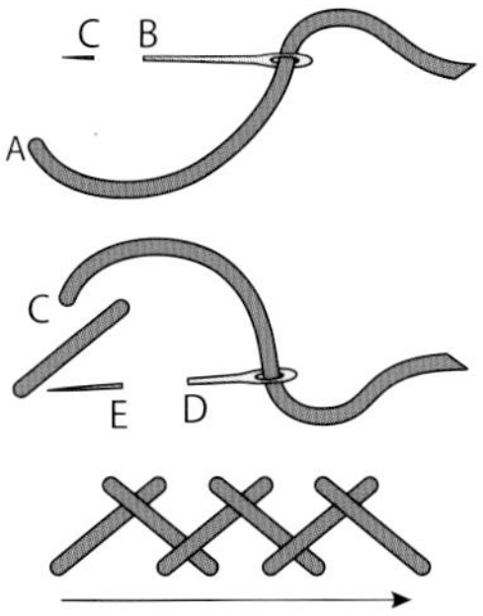

OVERSTITCH ZIGZAG

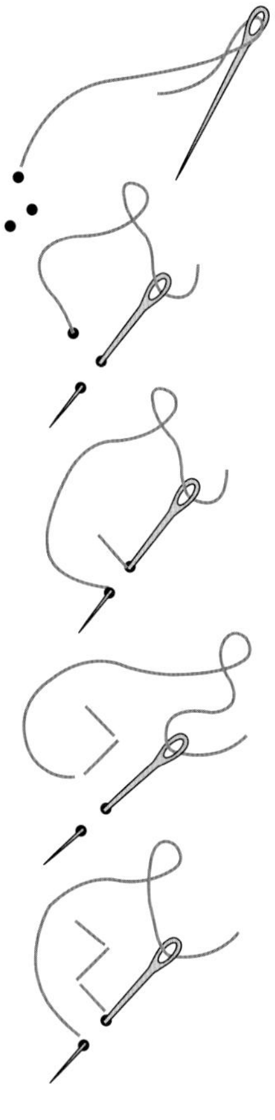

RUNNING STITCH

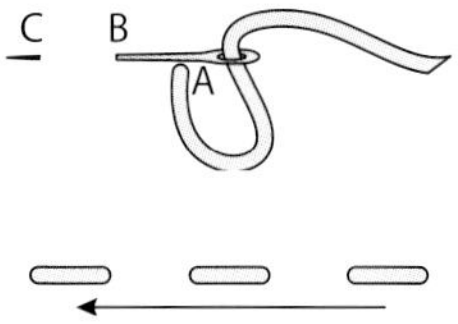

SATIN STITCH

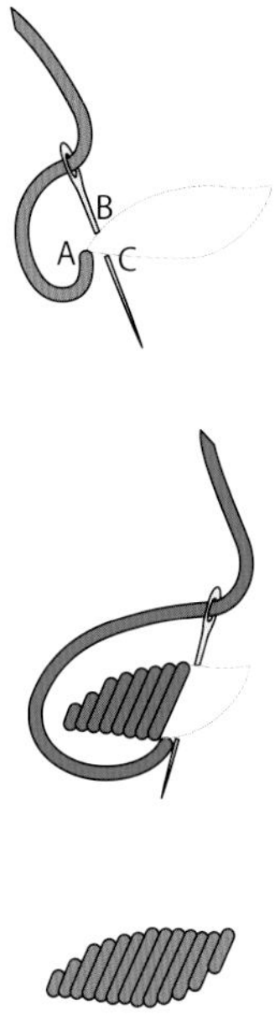

STEM STITCH

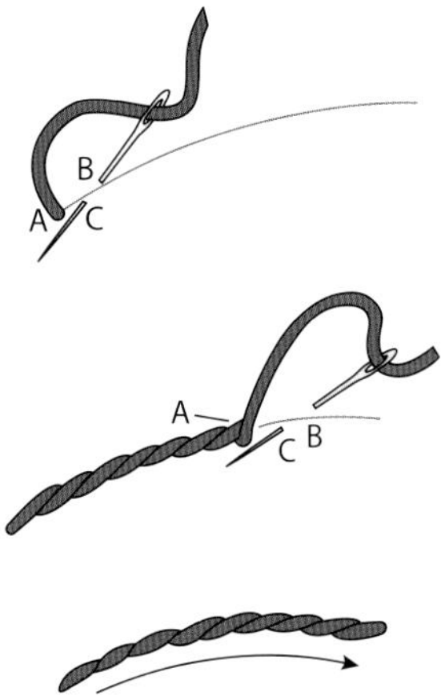

TAILOR TACKS

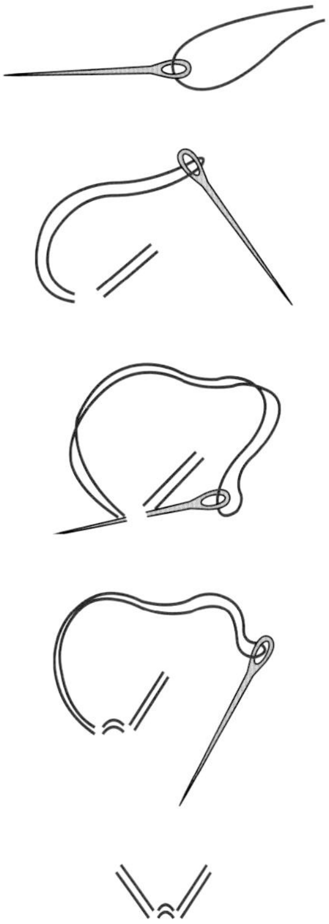

WHIPSTITCH

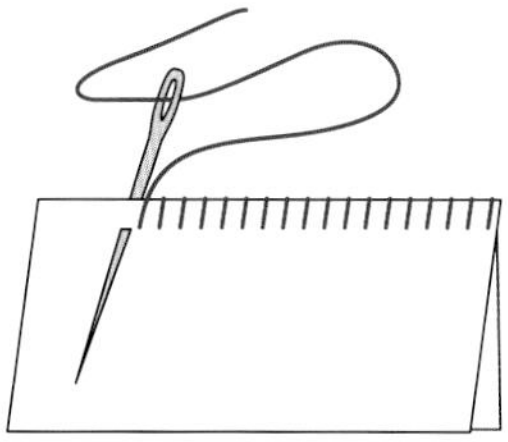

Projects

A Bit of a Hoot

Finished size: 30½″ × 39½″ (77cm × 100cm)

As the name *A Bit of a Hoot* implies, this is a small quilt that echoes the whimsical feeling of *Hooterville* (page 15) with little creatures of the night. As such, it is a great starting point to try out the techniques in this book.

In this quilt, the sky blue for the background glows against the dark brown tree, reminiscent of twilight. The creatures in this quilt are quite Australian, with the ringtail possum, the pygmy possum, and the echidna. If you want to have a feeling of your home, simply swap these creatures for the ones that come out to play in your backyard as night falls.

The owls have a slightly different look from the *Hooterville* owls. You can change their personalities by moving the eyes up or down or closer together. Three little bees are buzzing around, collecting their pollen before nightfall.

Make up all your little creatures and then play with them on different backgrounds until you find the right combination for you.

MATERIALS

Yardage is based on 44″ (112cm) wide fabric, unless otherwise noted.

Blue mottled print: 1 yard (1m) for background

Dark brown print: 1 yard (1m) for border/tree

Brown/blue dots: ⅜ yard (34cm) for binding

Wool or wool felt: 15 pieces 8″ × 12″ (20cm × 30cm) of different colors, including lime, dark green, and light green

Circle prints: 12–14 small pieces of different prints for flower centers and owl eyes

Paisley print: scrap containing 1 motif for bird wing

Batting: 36″ × 45″ (92cm × 115cm)

Backing: 2 yards (1.8m)

Perle cotton thread: size 8 or 10 in a variety of colors, including brown

CUTTING

Background

Cut 1 piece 31½″ × 41½″.

Border/tree

Cut 1 piece 31½″ × 41½″.

Binding

Cut binding as needed for your preferred binding style.

Appliqué pieces

Copy A Bit of a Hoot *appliqué patterns (pages 73–75) at 100%. The patterns give you the shapes to cut, and the pattern pieces show suggested stitching. I don't always specify the exact number of pieces to cut, as this is your opportunity to make the project your own.*

Note: *For cotton fabrics, trace around the freezer paper and cut out with a ¼″ seam allowance, then see the technique in Needle-Turn Appliqué (page 7). For wool or wool felt, there is no need to trace around the pattern or leave a seam allowance.*

1. Trace the appliqué patterns onto the dull (paper) side of freezer paper and cut on the drawn lines.

2. Press the freezer-paper templates onto the right side of the appropriate fabric.

3. Refer to the project photo to determine how many of each appliqué piece to cut. You may want more or less than shown in the photo. Cut the appliqué pieces.

4. Cut strips ⅜″ × 12″ for the stems—you will need 3 lime green, 5 dark green, and 3 light green.

5. Cut circles for the eyes and flower centers from the circle prints—2 pairs of circles for the owl eyes, 13 flowers/circles for the flower centers, and 1 paisley motif for the bird wing.

Make the Background

1. Place the brown fabric right side up on a table or the floor. Use a chalk pencil to mark off the sides, top, lower border, and central tree trunk.

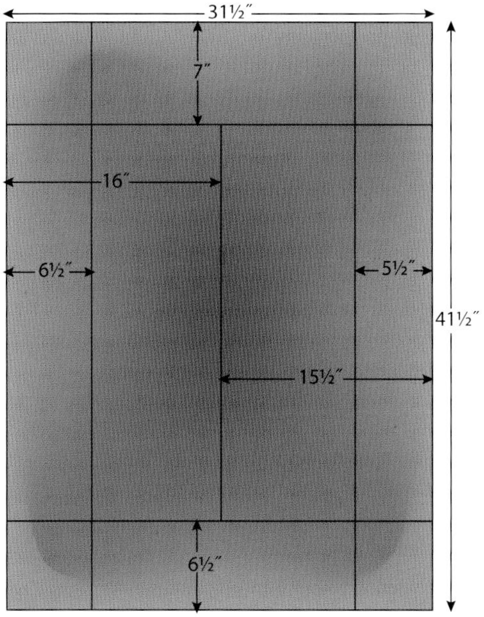

Mark background for tree.

2. Draw in the branches on the marked brown fabric, using the diagram and project photo (page 11) as a guide. Start by drawing lines and then make the branches thicker. Add some stumps at intervals along the branches so you can place leaves on them later.

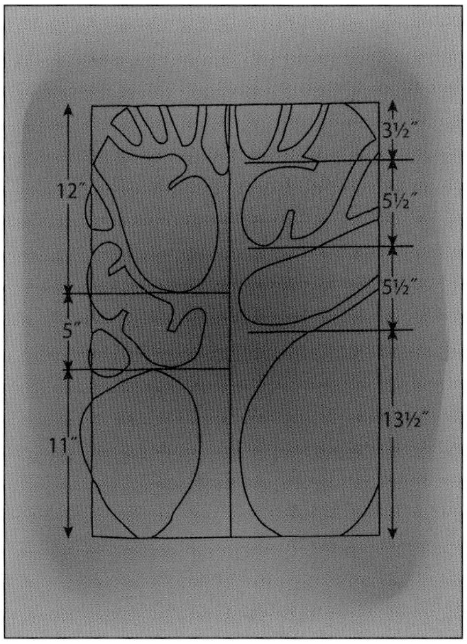

Freehand-drawn tree trunk and branches

3. Place the blue fabric right side up on the table or floor; then place the brown fabric right side up over the blue background and carefully pin together the 2 layers. You may need to tape the blue background to the floor or table first.

4. Use safety pins around the 4 outer edges to secure them together. Pin the tree branches using appliqué pins within the tree and branch areas.

5. Tack the tree to the background by stitching in the tree and branch area only. Use safety pins to hold the 2 layers together outside the tree.

6. Appliqué the tree to the background using needle-turn appliqué with a running stitch (page 9). Stitch close to the turned edge, trimming away the brown fabric as you go and leaving a ¼″ seam allowance. On corners and inward curves, it may be necessary to do a small stitch over the edge to hold the fabric securely.

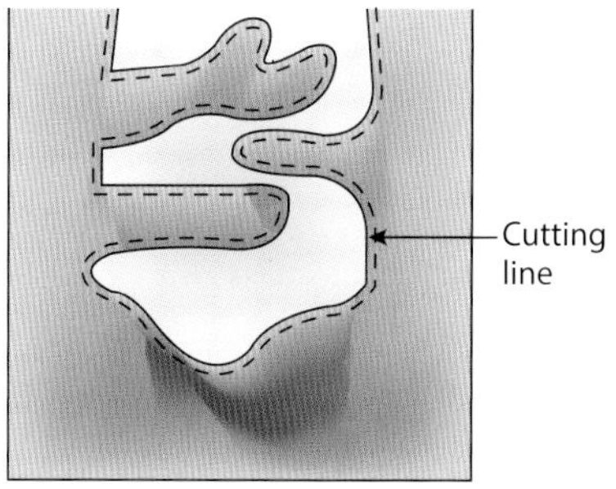

Cut just outside drawn line.

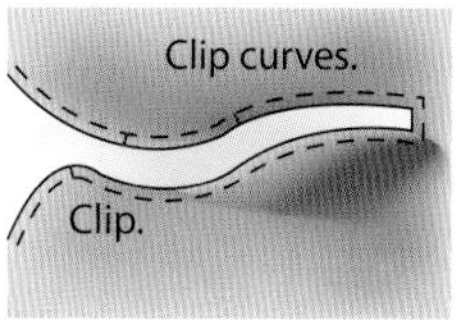

Clip curves as needed.

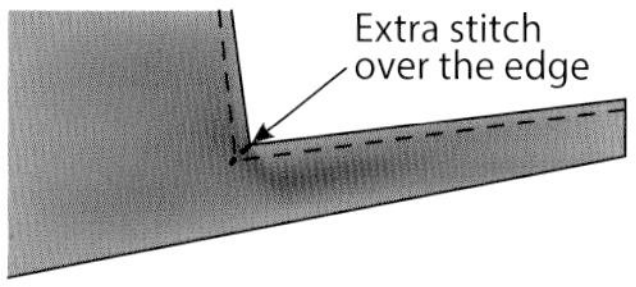

Use extra stitch in inward corners.

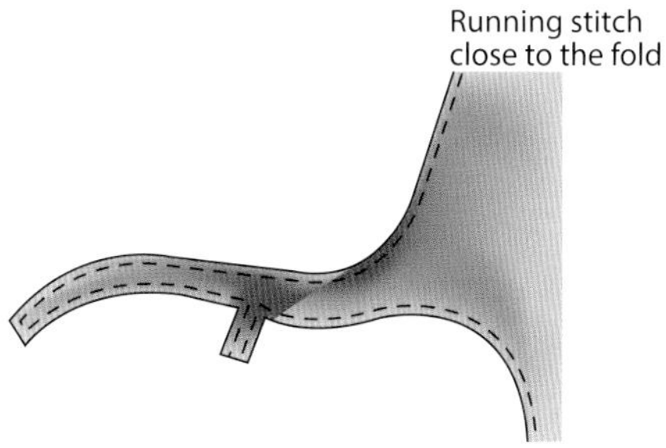

Stitch with running stitch close to fold.

7. Continue stitching until you have completed the whole tree. I left the blue background under the tree to give the tree more substance. If you wish, you may trim it away.

Appliqué

Note: *I like to stitch as much of the appliqué as I can before I apply it to the background. Refer to Appliqué Basics (page 5) and Embroidery Stitches (page 9) as needed.*

Owls

1. Pin and whipstitch the wings over the body, overlapping ½″.

2. Needle-turn the fabric for the eyes onto the body.

3. Stitch the beak with a whipstitch.

4. Stitch the owls together, adding the needle-turned fabric eyes.

5. Pin the hood over the face and eyes and stitch with a running stitch.

Birds

Stitch the bird wings, referring to the photo (below) for guidance. Add the eyes with small circles of felt and then attach the beaks.

Leaves

Stitch the center pieces to the leaves, using a variety of embroidery stitches.

Flowers and Stems

Needle-turn the fussy-cut circles onto some wool. Cut the flower shapes to reflect the center shapes, using the patterns as a guide.

Add All the Shapes to the Background

To arrange all the appliqué pieces on the background, it is helpful to use a design wall (page 8). If you don't have access to one, you can use a table or even the floor. Use the project photo (page 11) as a guide for placement.

Note: *When placing your shapes, remember that there is a ½″ margin around the background outside edge to allow for trimming and a seam allowance.*

1. Position the owls on the branches and pin them in place with appliqué pins. Whipstitch in place.

2. Position the flowers along the lower edge and sides of the quilt top, adding stems and leaves as desired. The straight strips for the stems will curve easily to the desired shape. Cut the strips to the length you need as you go, and then add the leaves and animals.

3. Stitch the shapes in place using any of the embroidery stitches (page 9).

4. Pin and stitch 3 yellow circles to the background for the bees. Use black cotton and large whipstitches to stitch the bees' stripes. Use large chain stitches to stitch the wings.

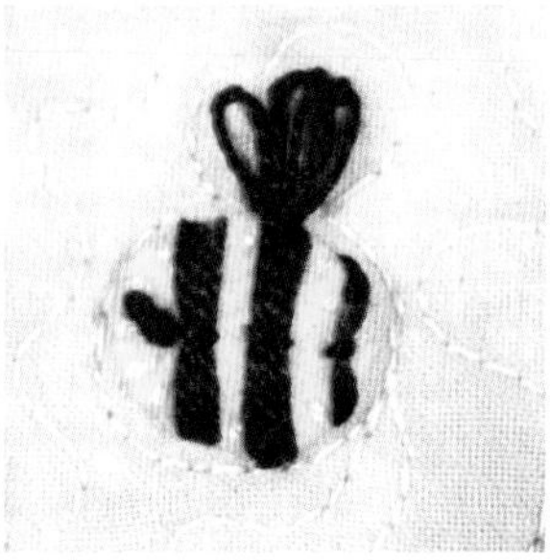

Finish

1. Trim the top to 30½″ × 39½″.

2. Layer, baste, and quilt as desired. I machine-quilted using stippling on the blue background, and then I outlined around all the appliqué and tree shapes. I used a more open machine quilting on the tree so that it would stand out from the background.

3. Use your preferred method to bind the edges.

Hooterville

Finished size: 42½″ × 52″ (108cm × 132cm)

Hooterville was the first quilt that I made using wool. This is where the love affair began. This quilt is full of colorful images of the night garden, including happy little birds tweeting on branches and owls casting a playful eye over the surroundings. Flowers and leaves decorate the forest floor. (If you want a smaller quilt to start with, try *A Bit of a Hoot*, page 11.)

My idea was to have a background that represents the colors of early evening, with appliqué that contrasts with a neutral background. I think this quilt would work equally well using other, more colorful backgrounds in plains or subtle prints. If you want to change the colors, try auditioning all of the leaves, flowers, birds, and owls on different backgrounds. It is a fun quilt! Let your imagination go as you enjoy the freedom that working with wool gives you.

I used linen for the background in my quilt, because I find it is beautiful to do handwork on linen's more open weave. Alternatively, you could use solid homespun.

As you select your fabrics, remember that the leaves don't need to be true-to-life green. You can achieve a quirky look by using unreal colors in real shapes. For your creatures, look for fabrics that jump off the bolt, with swirly lines for eyes, paisley prints for tails, and circular patterns for flower centers. The process of looking for detail in your fabrics will open your eyes to new ways of using what is at hand.

MATERIALS

Yardage is based on 44″ (112cm) wide fabric, unless otherwise noted.

Black linen, 55″ (140cm) wide: 2 yards (1.8m) for background and binding

Gray linen, 55″ (140cm) wide: 1½ yards (1.4m) for background

Wool or wool felt: 20–22 squares 10″ × 10″ (25cm × 25cm) in a variety of colors

Fabric pieces for fussy cutting: circles for flowers and owl eyes, paisleys for bird tails and dragonfly wings, and mirror-image patterns for butterfly wings

Batting: 50″ × 60″ (127cm × 152cm)

Backing: 3 yards (3m)

Perle cotton thread: size 8 or 10 in a variety of colors

CUTTING

Black linen

Cut 1 piece 43½″ × 53″.

Cut the remaining fabric for binding as needed for your preferred binding style.

Gray linen

Cut 1 piece 43½″ × 53″.

Appliqué pieces

Copy the Hooterville *appliqué patterns (pages 76–83) at 100%. The patterns give you the shapes to cut, and the pattern pieces show suggested stitching. I don't always specify the exact number of pieces to cut, as this is your opportunity to make the project your own.*

Note: *For cotton fabrics, trace around the freezer paper and cut out with a ¼″ seam allowance, then see the technique in Needle-Turn Appliqué (page 7). For wool or wool felt, there is no need to trace around the pattern or leave a seam allowance.*

1. Trace the appliqué patterns onto the dull (paper) side of freezer paper and cut on the drawn lines.

2. Press the freezer-paper templates onto the right side of the appropriate felt or fabric. Refer as needed to Appliqué Basics (page 5) for specific information on suggested fabrics for the appliqué pieces.

3. Cut the wings, ears, nose, and feet from wool felt.

4. Using the project photo (page 15) as a guide, cut enough leaves from wool to add at the stumps on the branches and the branch ends. I used approximately 40 leaves on my tree.

5. Cut the birds from wool felt.

6. Cut the dragonfly, the worm, and the butterfly from wool. Cut some woven fabrics for the wings to be needle-turned.

7. Fussy cut some print fabrics for the flower centers to needle-turn onto some wool. Cut the flower shapes to reflect the center shapes, using the patterns as a guide.

8. Cut the stems and leaves from wool, keeping the edges (as much as possible) on the bias grain to reduce frayed edges.

Make the Background

1. Place the black linen right side up on a table or the floor. Use a chalk pencil to mark off the sides, top, and lower border. Use these lines as guides when drawing the branches.

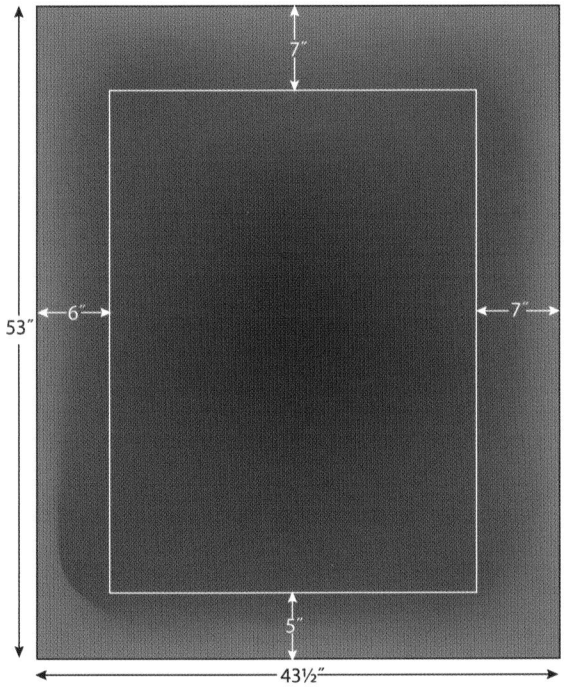

Mark fabric for tree.

2. Draw in the branches on the marked black linen, using the diagram and project photo (page 15) as a guide. Start by drawing lines and then make the branches thicker. Add some stumps at intervals along the branches so you can place leaves on them later.

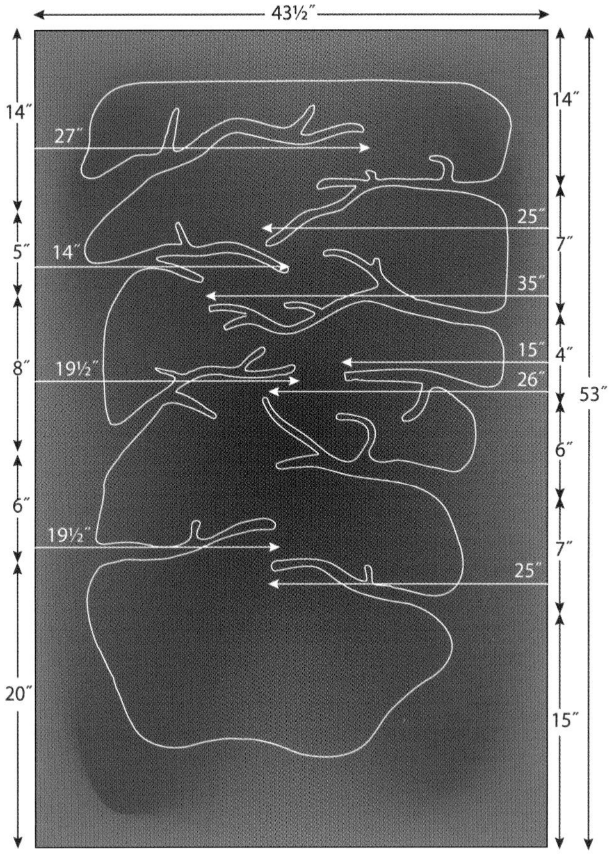

Freehand-drawn tree branches.

3. Place the gray background right side up on the table or floor. Place the black linen right side up over the gray background and carefully pin together the 2 layers. You may need to tape the gray background to the floor or table first.

4. Use safety pins around the 4 outer edges to secure them together. Pin the tree branches using appliqué pins within the tree and branch areas.

5. Tack the tree to the background by stitching in the tree and branch area only. Use safety pins to hold the 2 layers together outside the tree.

6. Appliqué the tree to the background using needle-turn appliqué with a running stitch (page 9). Stitch close to the turned edge, trimming away the black fabric as you go and leaving a ¼″ seam allowance. On corners and inward curves, it may be necessary to do a small stitch over the edge to hold the fabric securely.

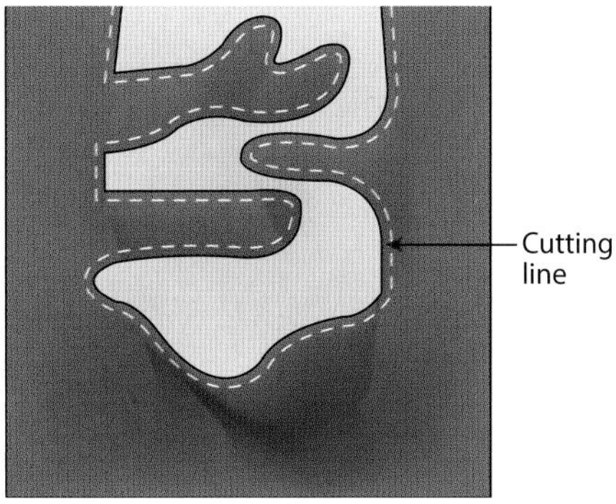

Cut just outside drawn line.

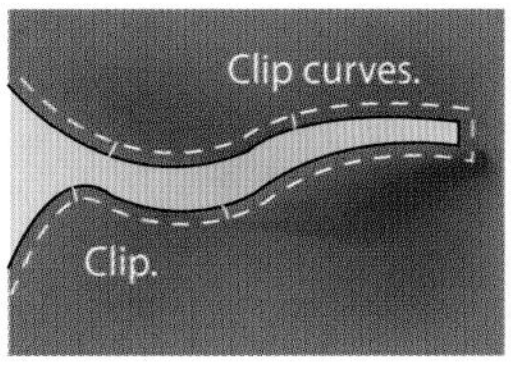

Clip curves as needed.

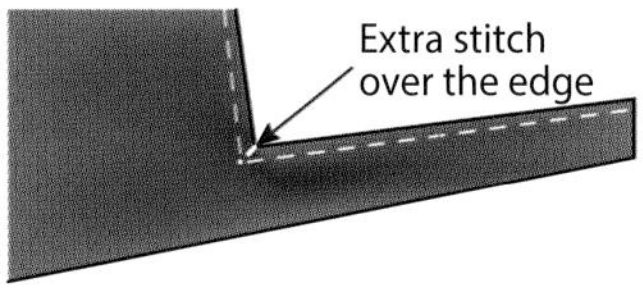

Use extra stitch in inward corners.

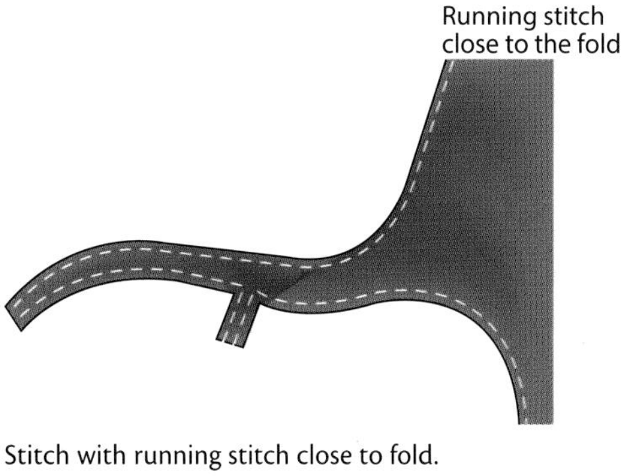

Stitch with running stitch close to fold.

7. Continue stitching until you have completed the whole tree. I left the gray background under the tree to give the tree more substance. If you wish, you may trim it away.

Appliqué

Note: *I like to stitch as much of the appliqué as I can before I apply it to the background. Refer to Appliqué Basics (page 5) and Embroidery Stitches (page 9) as needed.*

When placing your shapes, remember that there is a ½″ margin around the background outside edges to allow for trimming and a seam allowance.

Owls

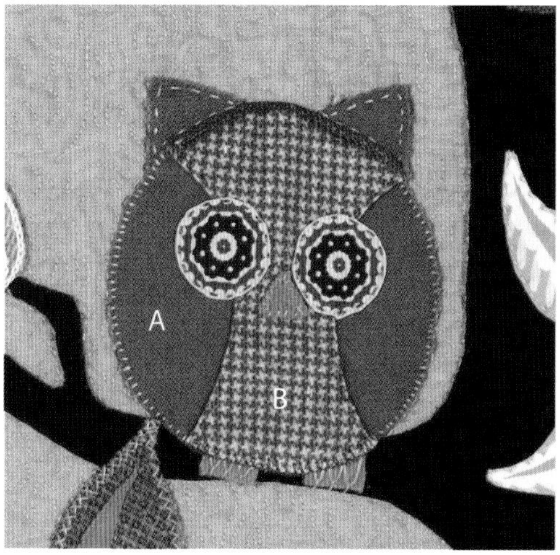

1. Cut the owl body A from wool felt.

2. Cut B from cotton fabric, allowing a ¼″ seam allowance around the template. Needle-turn the long edges with running stitch and stitch to the body.

3. Pin the owls together, overlapping the body ½″ over the wings. Needle-turn the top (head) and lower body. Whipstitch the wings and nose onto the owl.

4. Cut 2 circles for the eyes and needle-turn them in place. You can change the owl's personality by the position of the eyes. To emphasize the eyes, I outlined them with a row of chain stitch and added French knots in the center.

5. Pin the owls into position on the branches. Tuck the ears under the head ¼″ and then stitch the owl in place, needle-turning the top (head) and lower body. Use big stitches to stitch the feet.

Leaves

1. Add some scrap bits to the center of the leaves to add dimension. Add as much stitching as you like—the more, the merrier.

2. Pin the leaves in place over the stumps and branch ends. Add one leaf at a time and arrange them as you go. Refer to the project photo (page 15) for placement, leaving some space to add the birds and the dragonfly.

3. Stitch the leaves in place using any of the stitches shown. Or you may like to make up some stitches.

Birds

1. Fussy cut some pieces from the printed fabrics for the wings and needle-turn them in place over the bird bodies.

2. Add some small wool circles for the eyes and complete them with a French knot in the center.

3. Decorate the birds with some extra embroidery stitches.

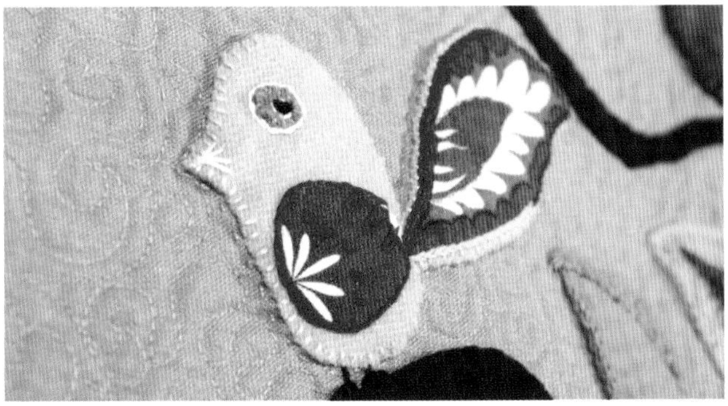

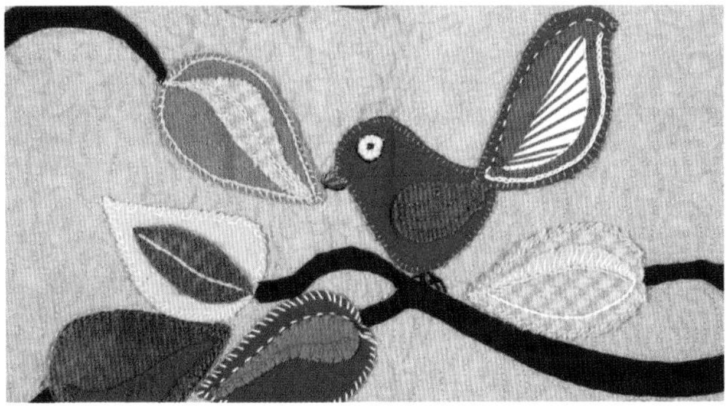

Dragonfly and Butterfly

1. If you used woven fabrics for the wings, needle-turn the pieces into place. If your fabrics differ a lot from mine, you may need to alter the body shapes.

2. Whipstitch the pieces in place and decorate as desired with extra embroidery. Add little wool circles for the eyes and antennae.

3. Place the birds, dragonflies, and butterfly around the tree's top and sides. Whipstitch in place.

Flowers and Worm

1. Position the flowers along the lower edge and sides of the quilt top, adding the stems and leaves as desired.

2. Whipstitch the wool felt pieces.

3. Decorate the pieces with embroidery.

4. Add the worm to the tree trunk.

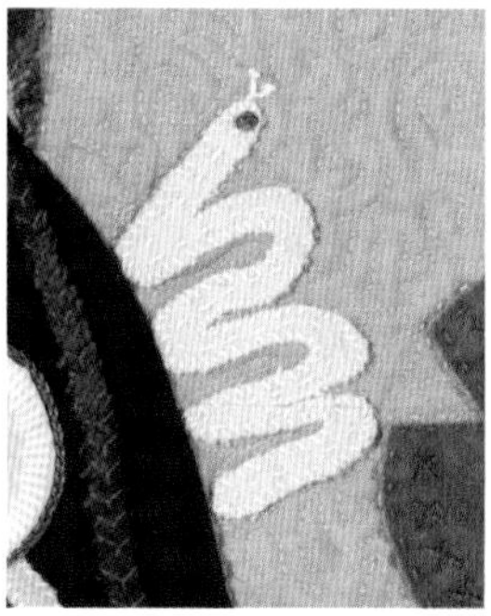

Finish

1. Trim the top to 42½″ × 52″.

2. Layer, baste, and quilt as desired. I machine-quilted using stippling on the gray background, and then I outlined around all the appliqué and tree shapes. I used minimal machine quilting on the tree so that it would stand out from the background. I outlined around the appliqué on the tree with black perle cotton.

3. Use your preferred method to bind the edges.

Birds on a Wire

Finished size: 45″ × 54″ (115cm × 137cm)

Birds on a *Wire* was inspired by the view from my back veranda. I live ten minutes from the center of a large city, and yet we have a wide range of birds that live in the big trees that surround my home. I am always fascinated by the number of birds that rest on the overhead power lines when there are so many beautiful trees to choose from.

Seeing the birds from a distance in my yard, I can just see the silhouettes of the birds and all the crazy poses they make. Looking at the finished quilt, I can almost hear their singing and squawking conversations as they hang on the lines.

For this quilt, I chose newsprint for the background, which in hindsight seems to represent the daily conversation between the birds. The black silhouettes contrast nicely with the background, though it would work equally well with other small prints. You may like to make your birds in bright colors to represent your local wildlife. Either way, it is a bit of fun. The garden at the bottom is worked with long stems and leaves that reach up to the birds up above. The contrast in line adds interest to the finished composition.

The border for this quilt frames the scene with an instant splash of color. I used scraps from my basket for the Nine-Patch blocks. However, this is a great opportunity to treat yourself and buy a nice, bright selection of fabrics from your local store. Always good for the soul!

MATERIALS

Yardage is based on 44″ (112cm) wide fabric, unless otherwise noted.

Cream newsprint (or similar): 1⅛ yards (1.1m) for main background

Black newsprint (or similar): ¼ yard (25cm) for Border 1

Polka dots: ¾ yard (70cm) for Nine-Patch border blocks

Bright prints: ⅛ yard (12cm) of 10 different fabrics for Nine-Patch border blocks

Black iron-on bias tape: ¼″-wide 3½ yards (3.2m)

Black wool felt: 1 piece 8″ × 25″ (20cm × 65cm) for birds

Bright wool felt: 10 squares 8″ × 8″ (20cm × 20cm) of different colors for flowers

Green wool felt: 5 pieces 6″ × 16″ (15cm × 40cm) of different greens

Flower and circle prints: 20 different motifs for flower centers

Paisley prints: scraps of 2 different prints for leaves

Backing: 2¾ yards (2.5m)

Binding: ½ yard (45cm)

Batting: 49″ × 58″ (125cm × 147cm)

Perle cotton thread: size 8 in a variety of colors, including black and yellow

CUTTING

Cream newsprint fabric

Cut 1 piece 34″ × 43″.

Polka dots

Cut 10 strips 2″ × width of fabric; subcut each strip into 3 strips 2″ × 13″.

Bright prints

Cut 10 strips 2″ × width of fabric; subcut each strip into 3 strips 2″ × 13″.

Black newsprint fabric

Cut 4 strips 2″ × width of fabric; subcut 2 strips 2″ × 42½″ and 2 strips 2″ × 36½″.

Note: *Piece as needed if your fabric is not at least 42½″ wide.*

Binding

Cut binding as needed for your preferred binding style.

Appliqué pieces

Copy the Birds on a Wire *appliqué patterns (pages 84–88) at 100%. The patterns give you the shapes to cut, and the*

pattern pieces show suggested stitching. I don't always specify the exact number of pieces to cut, as this is your opportunity to make the project your own.

Note: *For cotton fabrics, trace around the freezer paper and cut out with a ¼″ seam allowance, then see the technique in Needle-Turn Appliqué (page 7). For wool felt, there is no need to trace around the pattern or leave a seam allowance.*

1. Trace the appliqué patterns onto the dull (paper) side of freezer paper and cut on the drawn lines.

2. Press the freezer-paper templates onto the right side of the appropriate felt or fabric. Refer as needed to Appliqué Basics (page 5) for specific information on suggested fabrics for the appliqué pieces.

3. For stems: Cut 8 strips ⅜″ × 16″ from lime green, 5 strips ½″ × 16″ from dark green, and about 2 strips ⅜″ × 16″ from medium green. You may want to use more stems, maybe fewer.

4. Cut out the bird shapes from black wool felt. I used 19 birds.

5. From the flower and circle prints, fussy cut the shapes, allowing a ¼″ seam allowance for needle-turning.

6. From the paisley prints, fussy cut the shapes, allowing a ¼″ seam allowance for needle-turning.

Appliqué

Note: *I like to stitch as much of the appliqué as I can before I apply it to the background. Refer to Appliqué Basics (page 5) and Embroidery Stitches (page 9) as needed.*

Flowers

1. Needle-turn the fussy-cut circles and flowers to a piece of felt large enough for the flower.

2. After the fabric is attached, cut the flower, using either the patterned fabric as a guide or the flower patterns provided.

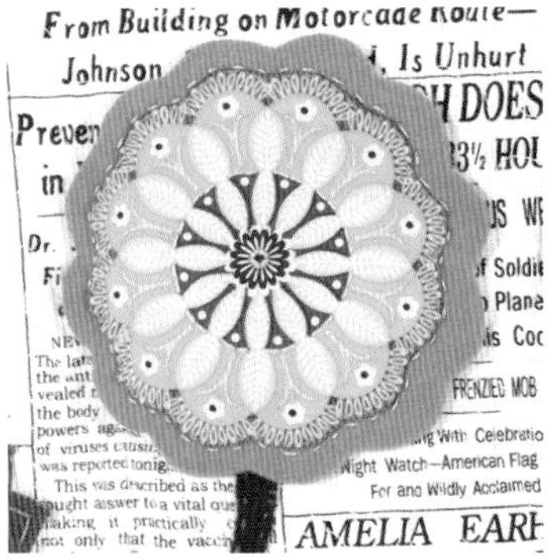

Leaves

1. Needle-turn the fussy-cut paisleys to a piece of green felt large enough for the leaf.

2. After the fabric is attached, cut the leaves, using either the patterned fabric as a guide or the leaf patterns provided.

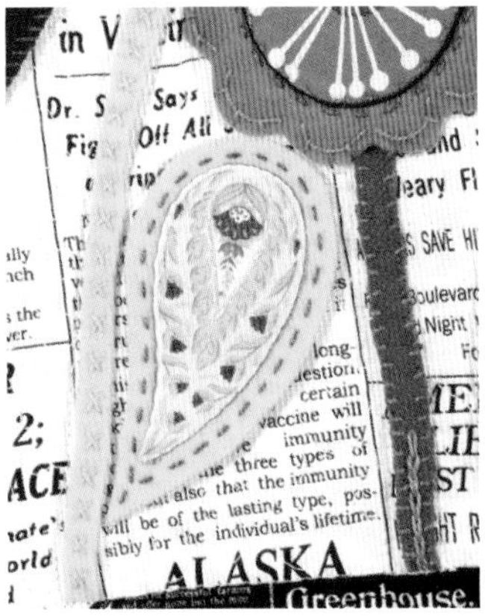

Make the Background

1. Pin and press the black iron-on bias tape to the cream print 34″ × 43″ piece, as shown in the diagram.

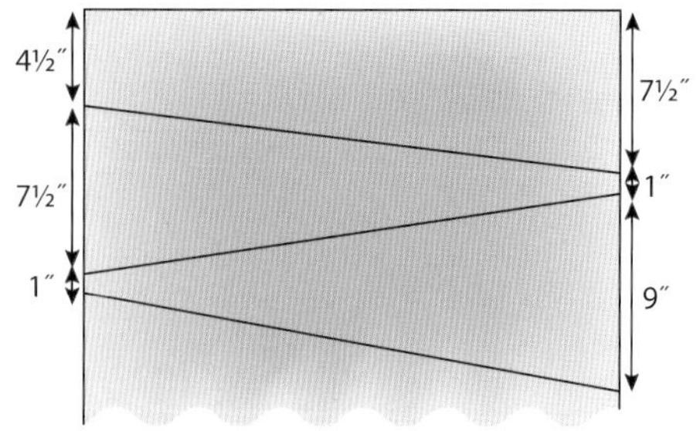

Placement for wires

2. Using black thread, machine stitch on both sides of the tape close to the edges.

3. Trim the background piece to 33½″ × 42½″.

4. Sew the black print 2″ × 42½″ strips to the sides of the background piece. Press the seams toward the black print.

5. Sew the black print 2″ × 36½″ strips to the top and bottom. Press the seams toward the black print.

Add All the Shapes to the Background

To arrange all the appliqué pieces on the background, it is helpful to use a design wall (page 8). If you don't have access to one, you can use a table or even the floor. Use the project photo (page 21) as a guide for placement.

When appliquéing the wool, you can use a vast array of embroidery stitches (page 9), including whipstitch, backstitch, running stitch, chain stitch, stem stitch, and zigzag. All stitches are done with perle cotton or similar.

Remember that there is a ½″ margin around the background outside edge to allow for trimming and a seam allowance. Allow for this when placing your shapes.

1. Place the stems on the lower edge of the background fabric. (The stems can extend into the seam allowance.) Then add the leaves and flowers. Move them around until you are happy with the layout in terms of balance and color.

2. Use appliqué pins to pin the wool to the background.

3. Stitch the stems, leaves, and flowers to the background using either matching or contrasting thread.

4. Place the birds on the wires, moving them around until you are happy with the layout. Pin the wool to the background using appliqué pins. Then whipstitch the birds in place with black cotton.

5. Pin and stitch 3 yellow circles to the background for the bees. Use black cotton and large whipstitches to add the stripes. Use large chain stitches to stitch the wings.

Make the Nine-Patch Blocks

Seam allowances are ¼″.

You need a total of 40 Nine-Patch blocks—20 of Block A and 20 of Block B.

1. Make 10 strip sets using 1 polka dot 2″ × 13″ strip between 2 matching bright print 2″ × 13″ strips. Press the seams toward the outside.

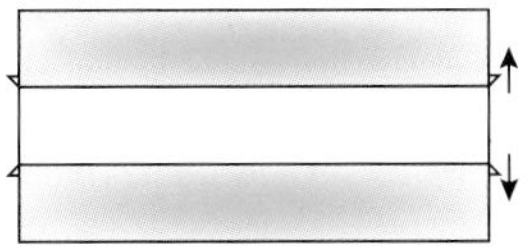

Make 10.

2. Make 10 strip sets using 1 bright print 2″ × 13″ strip between 2 polka dot 2″ × 13″ strips. Press the seams toward the center strip.

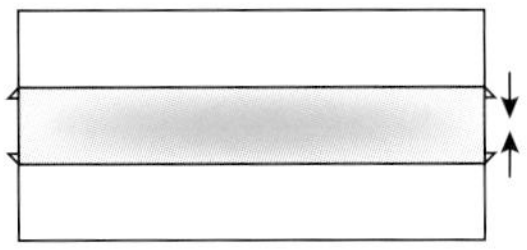

Make 10.

3. Crosscut all of the strip sets into 2″ sections, disregarding any leftover bits at the end of the strip. You will have a total of 120 sections.

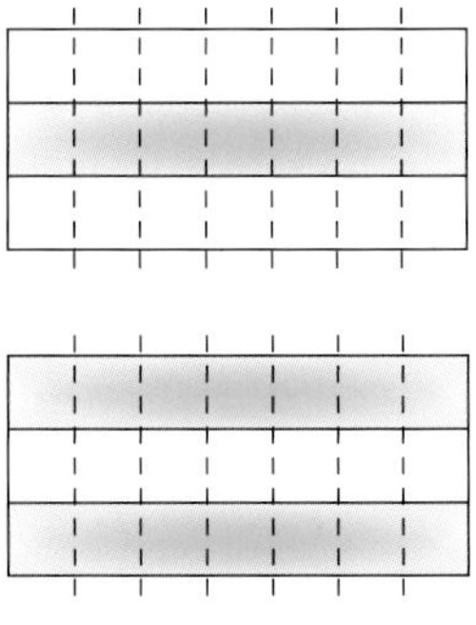

Cut strip sets into 2″ strips.

4. Arrange the sections into Nine-Patch blocks. Arrange 20 of Block A with a polka dot center patch and matching bright print patches. Arrange 20 of Block B with a bright print center patch and matching corner patches. You will have a total of 4 Nine-Patch blocks in each of 10 color combinations. Sew each block together.

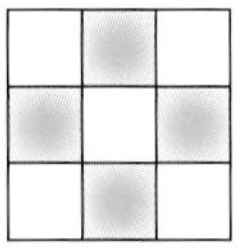

Block A—Make 20.

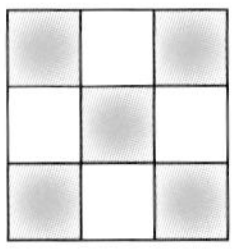

Block B—Make 20.

Assemble the Quilt

Seam allowances are ¼″.

1. Using a design wall (page 8) or table, arrange the Nine-Patch blocks around the quilt center alternating A and B blocks as shown. Refer to the quilt assembly diagram for guidance. You will need 10 blocks along each side and 10 blocks across the top and bottom. Spread out the different combinations of fabrics evenly and ensure that you keep the checkerboard pattern correct.

2. Stitch the 10 blocks together for each side. Press. Sew each border section to the sides of the quilt. Press the seams toward the black border.

3. Stitch the 10 blocks together for the top and bottom of the quilt. Press. Sew these border sections to the quilt. Press the seams toward the black border.

Quilt assembly diagram

Finish

1. Layer, baste, and quilt as desired. I machine-quilted using stippling on the background, and then I outlined around all of the appliqué. I used a walking foot to stitch close to the seam on either side of the black border. I did a more open machine quilting on the Nine-Patch border.

2. Use your preferred method to bind the edges.

Two's Company

Finished size: 42″ × 48″ (107cm × 122cm)

This is a great little quilt for children. It has all of the creatures of an African safari, and the quirky birds and fish complete the scene. It is fun making all the creatures and bringing them to life with their eyes and simple expressions. Play around with the background fabrics and simplify the borders if you wish. The colors you choose will transform the overall feel, from daylight to dusk, from summer to winter. The choice is up to you.

MATERIALS

Yardage is based on 44" (112cm) wide fabric, unless otherwise noted.

Center panel

Light green geometric: ¼ yard (23cm)

Medium green geometric: ⅛ yard (12cm)

Light green dot: ⅜ yard (35cm)

Yellow-green solid: ¼ yard (23cm)

Green stripe: ⅛ yard (12cm)

Black print: ⅛ yard (12cm)

Grass-green plain: ⅜ yard (34cm)

Border 1

Multicolor stripe: ⅛ yard (12cm)

Polka dots: ⅛ yard (12cm)

Blue stripe: ⅛ yard (12cm)

Border 2

Sky-blue stripe: ¼ yard (23cm)

Medium blue mottled: ¼ yard (23cm)

Bright aqua-blue solid: ¼ yard (23cm)

Aqua-blue check: ¼ yard (23cm)

Aqua-blue solid: ¼ yard (23cm)

Aqua-blue stripe: ¼ yard (23cm)

Mottled sea green: ¼ yard (23cm)

Dark sea green: ¼ yard (23cm)

Sea green: ¼ yard (23cm)

Gray-blue: ¼ yard (23cm)

Dark blue solid: ¼ yard (23cm)

Blue stripe: ¼ yard (23cm)

Border 3

Bright prints: ⅛ yard (12cm) each of 20–22 different prints for half-square triangles (You can use pieces from your scrap basket.)

Binding: ½ yard (45cm)

Wool felt: 20–22 squares 10" × 10" (25cm × 25cm) of different colors, including light green and olive green

Black wool felt: 1 piece 5" × 20" (15cm × 50cm)

Light green wool felt: 1 square 10" × 10" (25cm × 25cm)

Perle cotton thread: size 8 in a variety of colors

Backing: 2½ yards (2.3m)

Batting: 46" × 52" (117cm × 132cm)

CUTTING

Note: *Label each piece with the letter shown. The letters will be used in the construction steps.*

Center panel

Light green geometric: Cut 1 piece 4½" × 23½" (A).

Medium green geometric: Cut 1 piece 3" × 23½" (B).

Light green dot: Cut 1 piece 11" × 20½" (C).

Yellow-green solid: Cut 1 piece 8½" × 20½" (D).

Green stripe: Cut 1 piece 3½" × 19" (E).

Black print: Cut 1 piece 1½" × 25½" (F).

Grass-green solid: Cut 1 piece 8½" × 25½" (G).

Border 1

Multicolor stripe: Cut 1 strip 1½" × width of the fabric; subcut 1 strip 1½" × 25½" (H) and 1 strip 1½" × 19½" (K).

Polka dots: Cut 1 strip 1½″ × width of the fabric; subcut 1 strip 1½″ × 33½″ (I) and 1 strip 1½″ × 9½″ (M).

Blue stripe: Cut 1 strip 1½″ × width of the fabric; subcut 1 strip 1½″ × 14½″ (J) and 1 strip 1½″ × 18½″ (L).

Border 2

Sky-blue stripe: Cut 1 piece 5½″ × 6½″ (N).

Medium blue mottled: Cut 1 piece 5½″ × 13½″ (O).

Bright aqua-blue solid: Cut 1 piece 5½″ × 15½″ (P).

Aqua-blue check: Cut 1 piece 5½″ × 15½″ (Q).

Aqua-blue solid: Cut 1 piece 5½″ × 9½″ (R).

Aqua-blue stripe: Cut 1 piece 5½″ × 8½″ (S).

Mottled sea green: Cut 1 piece 6½″ × 9½″ (T).

Dark sea green: Cut 1 piece 4½″ × 6½″ (U).

Sea green: Cut 1 piece 6½″ × 13½″ (V).

Gray-blue: Cut 1 piece 6½″ × 13½″ (W).

Dark blue solid: Cut 1 piece 5½″ × 15½″ (X).

Blue stripe: Cut 1 piece 5½″ × 23½″ (Y).

Border 3

Bright prints for half-square triangles: Cut 86 squares 2⅞″ × 2⅞″.

Binding

Cut binding as needed for your preferred binding style.

Appliqué pieces

Copy the Two's Company *appliqué patterns (pages 89–99) at 100%. The patterns give you the shapes to cut, and the pattern pieces show suggested stitching. I don't always specify the exact number of pieces to cut, as this is your opportunity to make the project your own.*

Note: *For cotton fabrics, trace around the freezer paper and cut out with a ¼″ seam allowance to allow for needle-turn appliqué. For wool felt, there is no need to trace around the pattern or leave a seam allowance.*

1. Trace the appliqué patterns onto the dull (paper) side of the freezer paper and cut on the drawn lines.

2. Press the freezer-paper templates onto the right side of the appropriate felt or fabric.

3. Cut out all the appliqué pieces, referring to the project photo (page 26).

4. Cut the tree pieces from the black wool, cutting the branches along the lines provided.

Background and Borders

Seam allowances are ¼″.

Center Panel

Refer to the center panel diagram and stitch the following pieces together in this order: Sew light green geometric A to medium green geometric B. Then sew light green dot C to yellow-green solid D and add green stripe E. Stitch the A/B unit to the C/D/E unit. Stitch black print F to the bottom of the unit. Then stitch grass-green G to the bottom. Press.

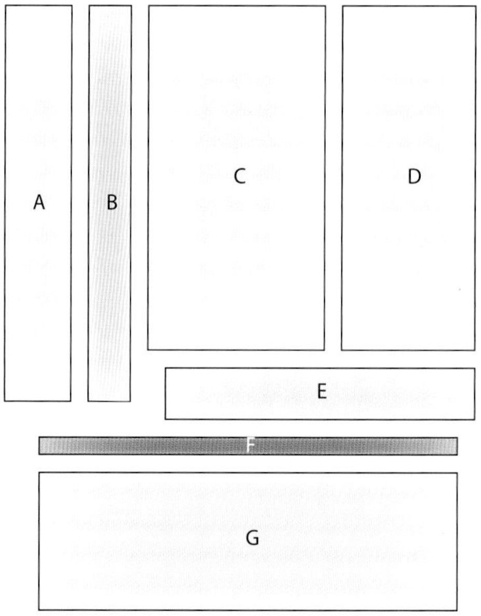

Center panel

Border 1

1. Refer to the border diagram to locate the narrow Border 1.

2. Stitch multicolor stripe H to the bottom edge of the center panel. Press the seam toward the border.

3. Stitch polka dot I to the right side. Press the seam toward the border.

4. Stitch blue stripe J to multicolor stripe K. Stitch this to the left side of the center panel. Press the seam toward the border.

5. Stitch blue stripe L to polka dot M. Stitch this to the top of the center panel. Press the seam toward the border.

Border 2

1. Refer to the border diagram to locate Border 2.

2. Stitch sky-blue stripe N, mottled medium blue O, and bright aqua-blue P together as shown. Stitch this border section to the right side of the quilt. Press the seam toward the center.

3. Stitch aqua-blue check Q, aqua-blue solid R, and aqua-blue stripe S together as shown. Stitch this border section to the top. Press the seam toward the center.

4. Stitch mottled green strip T, dark sea green U, sea green V, and gray-blue W together as shown. Stitch this border section to the left side. Press the seam toward the center.

5. Stitch dark blue solid X and blue stripe Y together as shown. Stitch this border section to the lower edge of the quilt. Press the seam toward the center.

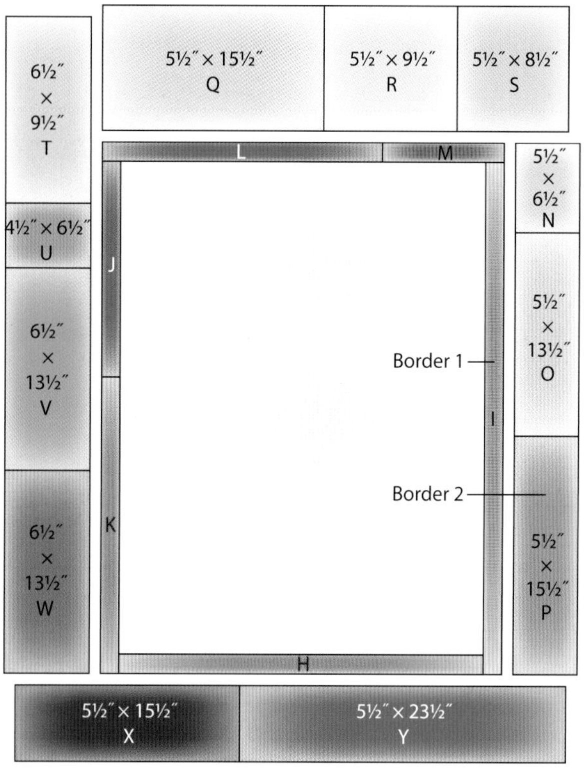

Borders 1 and 2

Half-Square Triangle Border

1. Stitch the half-square triangles as shown. Use all the bright print 2⅞″ × 2⅞″ squares to make a total of 86 half-square triangles.

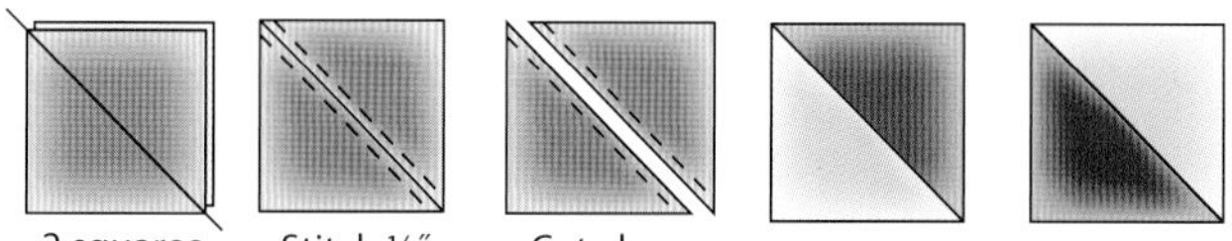

2. Stitch 2 rows of 22 units and 2 rows of 21 units. When stitching the units together, make sure that the diagonal line is always oriented the same direction. Press. Set these rows aside for now.

Appliqué

Note: *I like to stitch as much of the appliqué as I can before I apply it to the background. Refer to Appliqué Basics (page 5) and Embroidery Stitches (page 9) as needed.*

Stitch the spots, ears, eyes, and so on to the animals, birds, and fish. Use any stitches that you like. I stitched the eyes with a colonial knot in the center through all layers, and I stitched the spots with crosses.

Tree and Water

1. Place the tree on the background and splay out the branches. Place the green leaf pieces over the ends of the branches. You may need to cut back the branches until you have a balanced composition.

2. Pin the tree and branches in place on the background.

3. Stitch the tree with tiny whipstitches in matching thread. Backstitch the leaf sections to the background in matching colors.

4. Place the water on the background in the lower left corner. Stitch the water with backstitch.

Animals and Birds

1. Stitch the animals using any of the stitches. I mainly used a whipstitch. Decorate them with spots, stripes, and other markings.

2. Arrange the embroidered animals on the background. Pin them in place and appliqué as desired. Do not add the manes and hair to the lions, zebras, and giraffes until the quilting is done.

3. Pin and stitch the flamingos on the water and add the grass to fill the spaces. Stitch the grass with backstitch, running stitch, or whipstitch.

4. Pin and stitch the birds onto the tree and sky, using a variety of stitches.

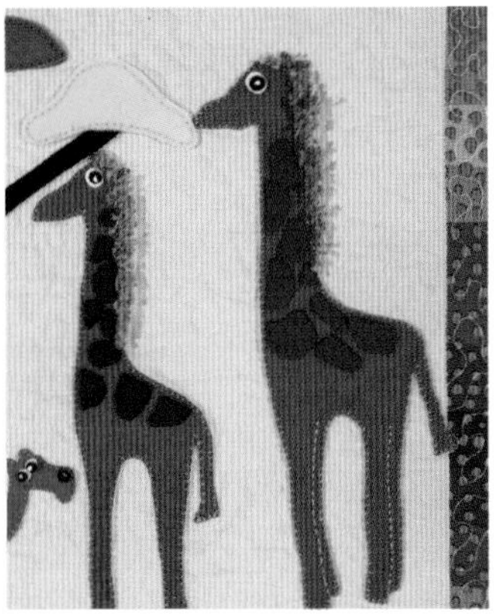

Fish

Pin and stitch the fish onto Border 2. Add some circle bubbles to fill the spaces. I stitched the bubbles with a large whipstitch in matching thread.

Finish

1. Refer to the project photo (page 26) to arrange the border rows of 22 half-square triangles to the sides of the quilt. Stitch the rows to the quilt center. Press the seams toward the center.

3. Arrange the border rows of 21 half-square triangles on the top and bottom and stitch to the quilt. Press the seams toward the center.

4. Layer, baste, and quilt as desired. I machine-quilted using stippling on the center background and outlined around all the appliqué and tree shapes. I quilted the water with bubbles and used long stippling for the sky. Don't forget to add the manes. They are done with lots of tiny tailor tacks (page 9).

5. Use your preferred method to bind the edges.

Overgrown

Finished size: 48″ × 61½″ (122cm × 156cm)

In Canberra in the springtime, there is an amazing festival called Floriade. Our nation's capital city comes to life with a sea of wonderfully colorful spring flowers. All of the parks and streets are planted with masses of spring blooms in colorful drifts. It is truly beautiful to see. This was my inspiration for *Overgrown*. I wanted to create the feel of Floriade, where all of the flowers are planted in both harmonious and contrasting colorways. This quilt has not only that beautiful punch of color but also the restful feel created by the curved lines. I was delighted with the result. It really does capture the feeling of Canberra in spring. In keeping with the playful theme, I had some of the flowers spill over the borders.

I chose red for the background, as I love the vibrancy of this color when splattered with the bright colors of the wool. You might like to choose another color that works with your decor or even a printed fabric. This quilt is a culmination of all of the stitches that I use with wool felt. It is a great way of creating a sampler as a teaching tool.

I hope you enjoy making this project as much as I did. For me, it became a challenge to come up with all the different ways that I could add the stems, leaves, and flowers while still keeping that contemporary feel.

MATERIALS

Yardage is based on 44″ (112cm) wide fabric, unless otherwise noted.

Red linen, 55″ (140cm) wide: 1 yard (1m) for background

Blue dots: ⅓ yard (30cm) for Border 1

Red print: 1⅛ yards (1m) for Border 2

Red/purple print: ½ yard (50cm) for binding

Wool felt: 26 squares 10″ × 10″ (25cm × 25cm) of 20 bright colors and 6 different greens

Perle cotton: size 8 in a variety of colors, including at least 3 greens

Backing: 3 yards (2.8m)

Batting: 52″ × 66″ (132cm × 168cm)

CUTTING

Red linen

Cut 1 piece 34″ × 47½″.

Blue dots

Cut 4 strips 2″ × width of fabric.

Red print

Cut 5 strips 6½″ × width of fabric.

Binding

Cut binding as needed for your preferred binding style.

Appliqué pieces

Copy the Overgrown *appliqué patterns (pages 100–105) at 100%. The patterns give you the shapes to cut, and the pattern pieces show suggested stitching. I don't always specify the exact number of pieces to cut, as this is your opportunity to make the project your own.*

Note: *All of the pieces are cut from wool felt, so there is no need to trace around the pattern to leave a seam allowance. As you cut out the appliqué pieces, note the row number for appropriate placement in the project.*

1. Trace the appliqué patterns onto the dull (paper) side of the freezer paper and cut on the drawn lines.

2. Press the freezer-paper templates onto the right side of the appropriate felt:

- Cut a number of flowers from the bright color felts. You can use the templates or cut freehand.
- Use a rotary cutter to cut a number of stems in each green by cutting straight strips ¼″–⅜″ wide of varying lengths.
- Cut the leaves from the corresponding green for each row.
- Cut the pieces for the dragonflies, bird, and bees.

Appliqué

Note: *I like to stitch as much of the appliqué as I can before I apply it to the background. Refer to Appliqué Basics (page 5) and Embroidery Stitches (page 9) as needed.*

1. Use the project photo (page 31) for guidance. Stitch all the flower circles before putting them on the background. You will need approximately 16 flowers in pink/orange, 14 in purple/mauve, 24 in yellow/cream, 20 in blue, 20 in cerise/purple, and 19 in orange/red.

TIP

As you go, you might like to make up some stitches and patterns of your own. The more variety you have, the more interesting it will look. On the smaller center circles, cut away a tiny circle in the center. This works like reverse appliqué, revealing the color of the background.

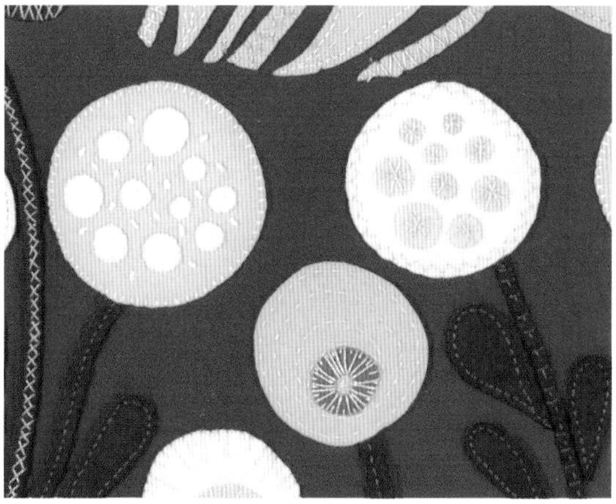

2. Place the red linen 34″ × 47½″ piece right side up on a flat surface. Refer to the background guide for the starting and ending position of the rows. Use a chalk pencil to mark the curved lines as a guide for the flower rows. When you are happy with the lines, stitch temporary lines over them using a light-colored perle cotton. (These guidelines will be removed at the end.)

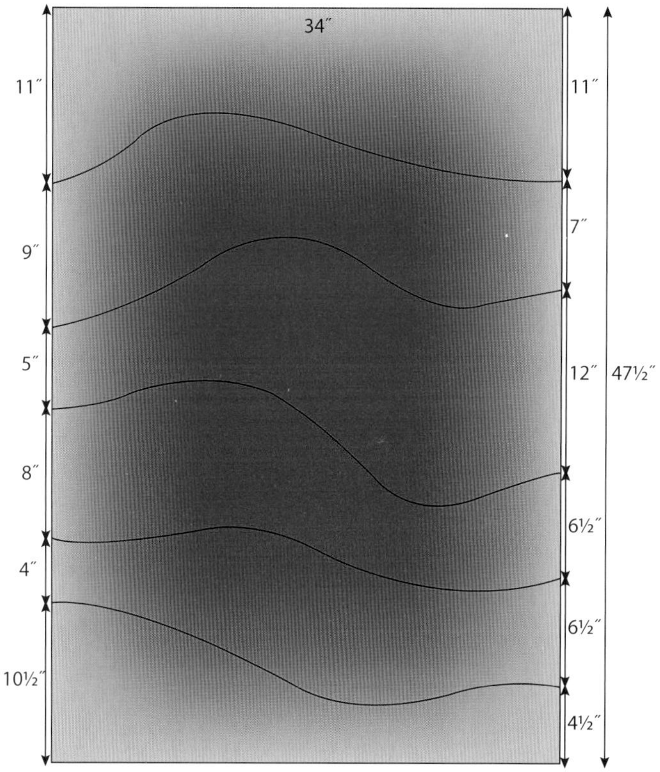

Background guide

3. Starting with Row 1, arrange the flowers on the background within the margins. Remember that there is a ½″ margin around the outside edge to allow for a seam allowance. Arrange the colors until you are happy with the placement. Place some stems so they are coming from the flowers to the next guideline for Row 2. Keep the stems curved to echo the garden's relaxed feel.

TIP

To keep the movement in this quilt, fill the space between each row as much as possible. Keep all the stems and most of the leaves touching the row below and try to keep most of the flowers touching the row above.

Note that some of the stems droop down with the flowers over the outside area. This keeps the garden looking more organic and less formal. When you remove the temporary guidelines at the end, you want to be able to see the curves created by each row. So be sure to set aside some of the flowers and stems to overlap the border area.

4. Place the leaves in between the stems and flowers.

5. When you are happy with the placement in Row 1, pin the stems, leaves, and flowers in place and stitch them to the background.

6. Work down the quilt with each color story from row to row, remembering to keep the design within the borders of each row.

Add the Borders

Seam allowances are ¼″.

1. Remove the stitched guidelines and press the quilt center lightly (try not to flatten the wool). Trim if necessary to 33½″ × 47″.

2. Remove the selvages of the blue dot 2″-wide strips, then stitch together the strips for Border 1. Press the seams open. Cut 2 pieces 2″ × 33½″ and 2 pieces 2″ × 50″.

3. Stitch the blue dot 2″ × 33½″ border strips to the top and bottom edges and press the seam toward the border. Stitch the blue dot 2″ × 50″ border strips to the sides and press the seams toward the border.

4. Remove the selvages of the red print 6½″-wide strips, then stitch the strips together for Border 2. Press the seams open. Cut 2 pieces 6½″ × 36½″ and 2 pieces 6½″ × 62″.

5. Stitch the red print 6½″ × 36½″ border strips to the top and bottom edges and press the seam toward the center. Stitch the red print 6½″ × 62″ border strips to the sides and press the seams toward the center.

6. Add the extra flowers and stems, spilling over onto the borders.

7. Add the bees and the dragonflies to fill any gaps.

Finish

1. Layer, baste, and quilt as desired. I machine-quilted using small stippling on the red background and the red print border. I machine-quilted the blue dot border with a swirl design. I used a walking foot to straight stitch around both sides of the blue dot border.

2. Use your preferred method to bind the edges.

Flowering Tree Runner

Finished size: 24″ × 53″ (63.5cm × 135cm)

My *Flowering Tree Runner* is a great little project that can easily be adapted to a larger quilt, a bed topper, or a pillow. The tree can be made using a small print in cotton as an alternative to the wool. Play around with backgrounds until you find one that suits your style. Remember that with the bright colors of the felt, you need to choose a background that allows the color to sing.

MATERIALS

Yardage is based on 44″ (112cm) wide fabric, unless otherwise noted.

White with small black dots: ½ yard (50cm) for background

Green mottled wool: ⅜ yard (35cm) for treetop

Black with large white dots: 1 fat quarter (18″ × 22″ or 46cm × 56cm) for tree trunk

Black print with green leaves: ⅜ yard (35cm) for Border 1

Bright prints: 25–28 strips 3″ × 10″–12″ (7.5cm × 25cm–30cm) lengths for Border 2 (These can be pieces from your scrap basket.)

Dotted print: ⅛ yard (12cm) for the tree flower centers

Circle prints: 10 motifs for flower garden centers

Small dotted print: 1 square 4″ × 4″ (10cm × 10cm) for bird's wing

Variety of wool felt: 12 squares 8″ × 8″ (20cm × 20cm) in a variety of bright colors, including blue for the bird

Green wool felt: 3 squares 8″ × 8″ (20cm × 20cm) of different greens

Black wool felt: 1 square 10″ × 10″ (25cm × 25cm)

White wool felt: 1 square 4″ × 4″ (10cm × 10cm) for bird's body

Binding: ⅜ yard (35cm)

Backing: 1¾ yards (1.6m)

Batting: 28″ × 57″ (71cm × 145cm)

Perle cotton threads: size 8 in a variety of colors, including black and green

CUTTING

White with dots

Cut 1 piece 43″ × 16″.

Green mottled wool

Cut 1 piece 12″ × 39″.

Black with white dots

Cut several tapering bias strips from the fat quarter as shown. Cut the strips wide enough that you can press under a ¼″ seam allowance on both sides of each strip. There is no need to be too accurate—trees have bumps and uneven branches. Refer to the project photo for reference. These bias strips will be intertwined together to form the tree trunk and then spread out for the tree branches.

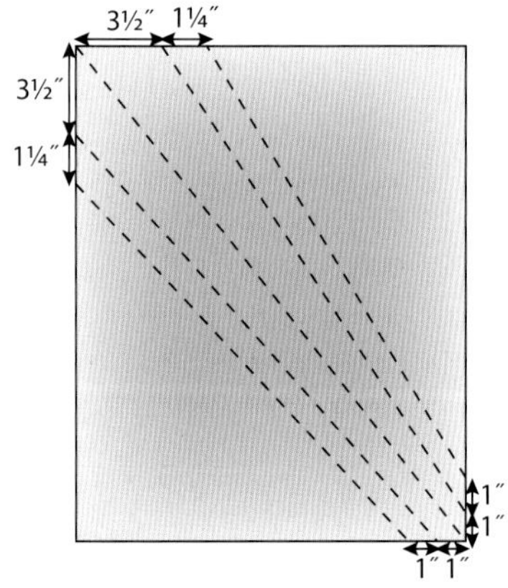

Mark and cut branches.

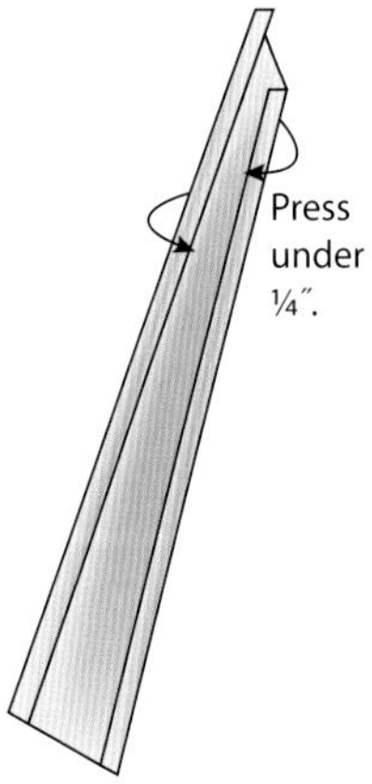

Turn under edges ¼″.

Border 1

Cut 2 strips 2½″ × width of fabric; subcut 2 strips 2½″ × 42½″.

Cut 1 strip 3½″ × width of fabric; subcut 2 strips 3½″ × 19½″.

Border 2

Cut approximately 90 pieces varying in sizes: 2″ × 3″, 2½″ × 3″, and 3″ × 3″.

Binding

Cut binding as needed for your preferred binding style.

Appliqué pieces

Copy the Flowering Tree Runner *appliqué patterns (page 106) at 100%. The patterns give you the shapes to cut, and the pattern pieces show suggested stitching. I don't always specify the exact number of pieces to cut, as this is your opportunity to make the project your own.*

Note: *For cotton fabrics, trace around the freezer paper and cut out with a ¼″ seam allowance, then see the technique in Needle-Turn Appliqué (page 7). For wool felt, there is no need to trace around the pattern or leave a seam allowance.*

1. Trace the appliqué patterns onto the dull (paper) side of the freezer paper and cut on the drawn lines.

2. Press the freezer-paper templates onto the right side of the appropriate felt or fabric.

3. Cut all the appliqué pieces. Refer as needed to the following suggestions for fabric for the appliqué pieces:

Dotted print: Cut approximately 33 circles, allowing ¼″ seam allowances for flower centers.

Small dotted print: Cut the wing, allowing a ¼″ seam allowance.

Green felt: Cut a number of leaves (mine has 46) from the 3 different colors of green. Use the pattern as a guide or simply cut them freehand.

Blue and white felt: Cut the bird body pieces.

Circle prints: Cut 10 flowers (circles), allowing a ¼″ seam allowance.

Black felt: Use a rotary cutter to cut a few ¼″-wide strips for the stems. Using the patterns provided, cut approximately 7 large leaves.

Appliqué

Note: *I like to stitch as much of the appliqué as I can before I apply it to the background. Refer to Appliqué Basics (page 5) and Embroidery Stitches (page 9) as needed.*

Green Treetop

1. See the green treetop in the project photo (page 35). Working on a flat surface, place the green mottled treetop 39″ × 12″ piece on top of the background 43″ × 16″ piece so that the top edges are aligned and both pieces are right side up. Center the treetop fabric right to left on the background.

2. Use a chalk pencil to draw the tree shape onto the fabric, using soft, deep curved edges. Refer to the photo as a guide. The green mottled treetop should come down just over halfway onto the background and should curve off to approximately 2″ from the top corners.

3. Cut out the treetop. If you are using cotton instead of wool, add a ¼″ seam allowance to needle-turn the edge.

4. Pin the treetop to the background and whipstitch it in place.

Tree Trunk

Pin the bias strips, entwining them below the treetop and spread them on top of the treetop. Needle-turn them in place on the background and treetop.

Flowers for the Tree

1. Needle-turn the dotted fabric circles to a piece of bright wool felt, stitching with perle cotton thread and small running stitches close to the folded edge.

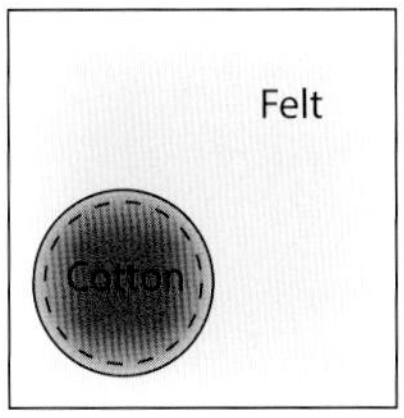

Needle-turn cotton fabric onto felt.

2. Cut out the felt circles, keeping a ⅜″ edge around the dotted fabric. (The circles don't need to be perfect; in fact, I think they look more organic if they are slightly uneven and not perfect.)

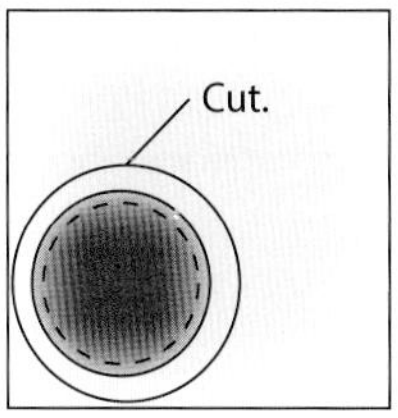

Cut out circle.

3. Place a circle from Step 2 onto another piece of felt and stitch again with perle cotton thread and a running stitch close to the edge. Cut again with a ⅜″ edge around the stitched circle.

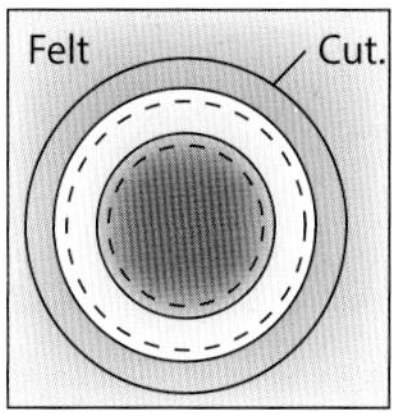

Stitch circle onto another piece of felt.

4. These are the flowers for the treetop. Set them aside for now.

Bird

1. Whipstitch the 2 pieces of the bird together, overlapping as indicated on the pattern.

2. Use a running stitch to needle-turn the wing to the bird.

3. Set the bird aside.

Flower Garden

1. Pin the flower garden centers to pieces of felt and needle-turn in place with a running stitch as in Step 1 of the flowers.

2. Cut the felt to echo the shape of the flower center, leaving at least ⅜″–½″ of the felt around the edge, depending on how large or small you want the flowers to be.

Add All the Shapes to the Background

To arrange all the appliqué pieces on the background, it is helpful to use a design wall (page 8). If you don't have access to one, you can use a table or even the floor. Use the project photo (page 35) as a guide for placement. When placing your shapes, keep in mind there is a ½″ margin around the outside edges of the background to allow for trimming and a ¼″ seam allowance.

1. On the background 43″ × 16″ section, arrange the treetop flowers, bird, and leaves on the tree until you are happy with the color placement. Keep a few leaves and flowers aside to overlap onto the border later.

2. When you are happy with the placement, pin everything in place with appliqué pins.

3. Stitch the leaves in place with small whipstitches in perle cotton.

4. Stitch the bird in place with small whipstitches.

5. Stitch the flowers in place with small running stitches and a variety of colors of perle cotton.

6. When the leaves and flowers are completed, scatter some small circles into the spaces and stitch them in place with 2 opposing crosses and a colonial knot in the center.

7. When the treetop is complete, arrange the garden flowers on the ground under the tree, playing with color and position. When you are happy with the placement, arrange the stems so that they gently curve from the flower head to the base, trimming the length of the stems as you go.

8. To complete the arrangement, scatter some leaves and pin them in place with appliqué pins.

9. Attach the flowers with a running stitch and perle cotton.

10. Stitch the leaves and stems with a running stitch in black perle cotton.

Add the Borders

Seam allowances are ¼″. Refer to the quilt assembly diagram.

Border 1

1. Trim the background center to measure 42½″ × 15½″, including seam allowances.

2. Stitch the black with green 2½″ × 42½″ Border 1 strips to the top and bottom of the runner. Press the seams toward the border.

3. Stitch the black with green 3½″ × 19½″ Border 1 strips to each side. Press the seams toward the border.

4. Stitch the extra flowers and leaves over the seam of the border.

Border 2

1. Randomly stitch the bright print 2″ × 3″, 2½″ × 3″, and 3″ × 3″ Border 2 pieces together into a strip at least 146″ long. Press the seams.

2. Cut the long pieced strip into 2 strips 3″ × 48½″ and 2 strips 3″ × 24½″.

3. Stitch the 3″ × 48½″ strips to the top and bottom edges and press the seams toward the center.

4. Stitch the 3″ × 24½″ strips to each side. Press the seams toward the center.

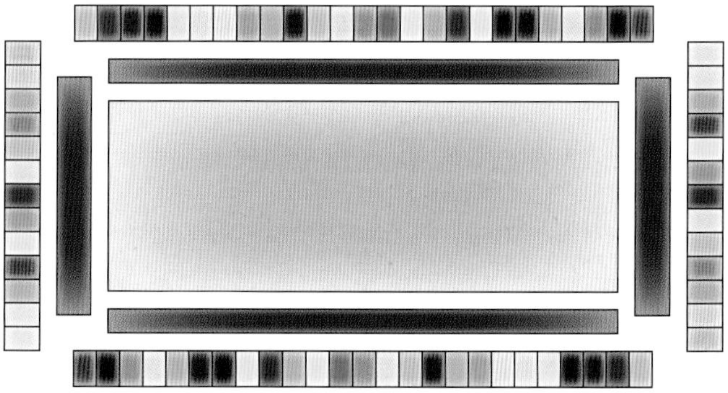

Quilt assembly diagram

Finish

1. Layer, baste, and quilt as desired. I machine-quilted my quilt, outlining around all of the shapes and stippling the background and bright print border. I stitched in-the-ditch on the straight lines of the borders.

2. Use your preferred method to bind the edges.

Clamshell Garden Runner

Finished size: 21″ × 50″ (53cm × 127cm)

I have always loved the idea of doing clamshells, but I know I will never get around to doing a whole quilt with them. I used them for the garden bed in this quilt, giving the shells a contemporary feeling by using modern fabrics and wool. The flower stems are swaying in the breeze, adding movement to the design. Search through your stash to find small flower and circle motifs for the flower centers. Audition different background fabrics using the guidelines in Backgrounds (page 8) to give a different look to your design.

MATERIALS

Yardage is based on 44″ (112cm) wide fabric, unless otherwise noted.

Cream word print: ½ yard (45cm) for background

Bright with dots: ¼ yard (25cm) for Border 1

Bright prints: 25–28 pieces 3½″ × 10″–12″ (9cm × 25cm–30cm) for Border 2 (These can be from your scrap basket.)

Circle prints: 37 motifs for flower centers

Cotton prints and wool felt for clamshells: 4″ × 8″ (10cm × 20cm) pieces in a variety of greens (These can be from your scrap basket.)

Wool felt: 12–14 squares 8″ × 8″ (20cm × 20cm) in a variety of bright colors

Green wool felt: 3 squares 10″ × 10″ (25cm × 25cm) of 3 different greens

3″ clamshell papers: 1 packet of at least 29 pieces, or make your own using the clamshell pattern (page 42)

Backing: 1½ yards (1.4m)

Binding: ⅜ yard (35cm)

Batting: 25″ × 54″ (64cm × 138cm)

Perle cotton threads: size 8 in a variety of colors, including green

Gluestick

CUTTING

Cream print

Cut 1 piece 13½″ × 42½″.

Circle prints

Cut approximately 37 circles, 1″–2½″ in diameter, with a ¼″ seam allowance.

Border 1

Cut 3 strips 1½″ × width of fabric; subcut 2 strips 1½″ × 15½″ and use the remaining to piece 2 strips 1½″ × 42½″.

Border 2

Cut approximately 85 pieces of bright prints in various sizes: 2″ × 3½″, 2½″ × 3½″, and 3″ × 3½″.

Binding

Cut binding as needed for your preferred binding style.

Appliqué pieces

Copy the Clamshell Garden Runner *appliqué patterns (page 42) at 100%. The patterns give you the shapes to cut, and the pattern pieces show suggested stitching.*

Note: *For cotton fabrics, trace around the freezer paper and cut out with a ¼″ seam allowance for the flower centers. However, for the clamshells, allow ⅜″. Follow the special instructions for seam allowances on the wool clamshell pieces.*

1. Trace the appliqué patterns onto the dull (paper) side of freezer paper and cut on the drawn lines.

2. Press the freezer-paper templates onto the right side of the appropriate felt or fabric.

3. Cut out all the appliqué pieces. Refer as needed to the following suggestions for fabric for the appliqué pieces:

Green felt: Cut a number of leaves (mine has 21) from the 3 colors of green felt. Use the pattern as a guide or simply cut them freehand. Use a rotary cutter to cut a variety of ¼″ strips for the stems.

Clamshell fabrics: Cut 29 clamshells from cotton or wool. When cutting from cotton, allow a ⅜″ seam allowance around the papers. When cutting from wool felt, you do not need to allow a seam allowance around the top curved edge, but do allow a ⅜″ seam allowance around the papers on the lower sections.

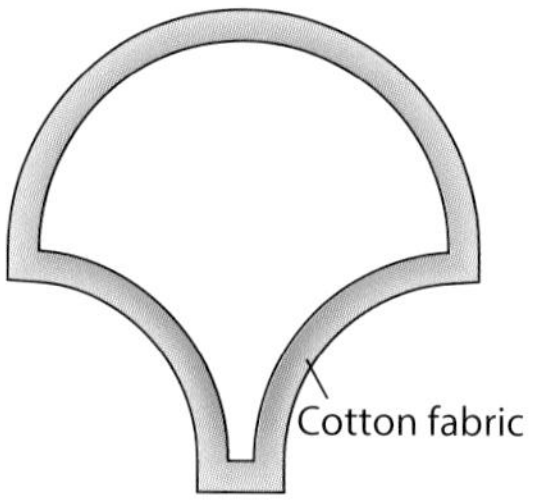

For cotton, allow ⅜″ allowance all around.

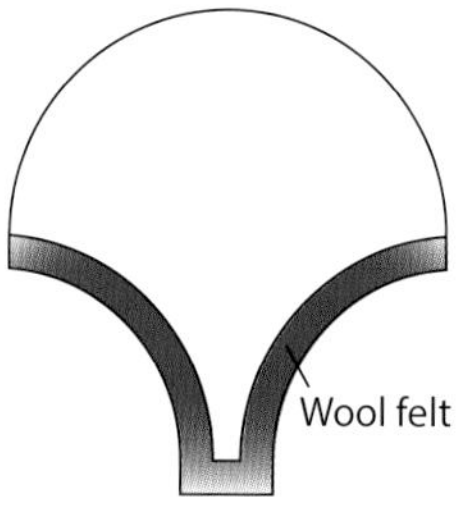

For wool, allow ⅜″ allowance around bottom portion only.

Prepare the Background

Use a chalk pencil or iron-out marking pen to mark a line 3″ from the lower edge of the background 13½″ × 42½″ piece. Mark the center along this line.

Appliqué

Note: *I like to stitch as much of the appliqué as I can before I apply it to the background. Refer to Appliqué Basics (page 5) and Embroidery Stitches (page 9) as needed.*

Clamshells

1. To prepare the cotton clamshells, apply a line of glue along the top, curved edge of the clamshell papers. Finger-press the cotton clamshells over the curved edge. Try to keep the edge smooth with no bumps. Press.

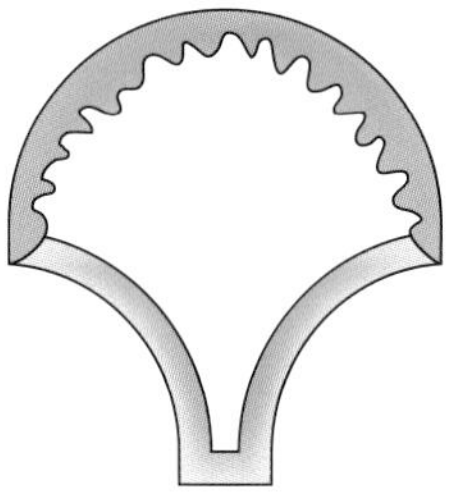
Glue fabric over paper.

2. Remove the papers and carefully re-press the clamshells.

3. Place the clamshell papers on the front of the clamshells and mark the points on the sides of the clamshell where the paper ends, as shown.

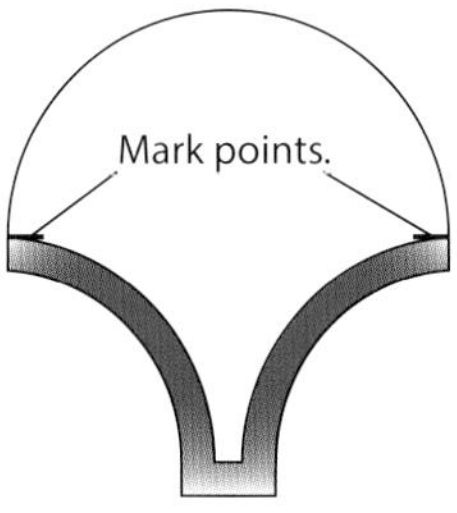

Mark points where paper ends.

4. Refer to the project photo (page 39) to arrange 14 clamshells on the background along the line, with the top edge of the clamshell touching the line. Starting from the center and working out toward the sides, position the clamshells so that the marked side points touch each other. Be sure to maintain the ¼″ seam allowance at each end of the background. Pin the clamshells in place.

5. Refer to the project photo to arrange the lower row of 15 clamshells beneath the top row. The top curve of the lower row should touch the points on the upper row, the side points on the lower row should meet, and the bottom row of clamshells should cover the raw edges of the clamshells in the row above. Pin the lower row of clamshells in place. (The points of the clamshells on the lower row will extend beyond the edge of the fabric.)

6. Tack the top row of clamshells to the background. Do not finalize the stitching on the top row of clamshells yet.

7. Stitch the lower row of clamshells to the background—use perle cotton thread and a small running stitch close to the top curved edge on the cotton clamshells and a whipstitch on the felt. Trim the lower row of clamshells even with the edge of the background fabric.

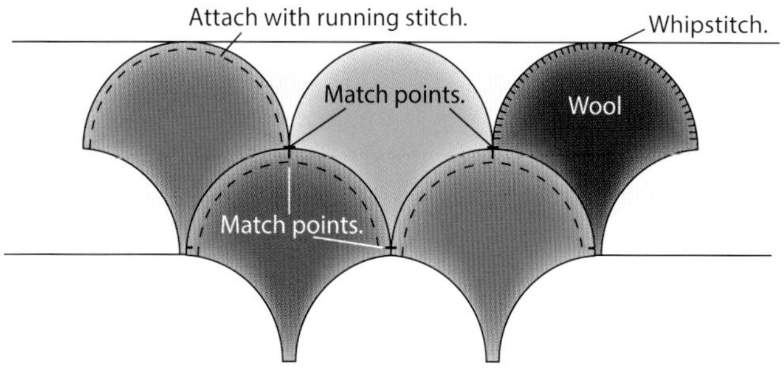

Arrange and pin clamshells on background.

Flowers

1. Refer to Needle-Turn Appliqué (page 7) to appliqué the dotted flower circles to a piece of bright wool felt. Stitch with perle cotton and a running stitch close to the folded edge.

2. Cut out the felt circles, keeping a ⅜″–½″ edge around the flower fabric. (The circles don't need to be perfect; in fact, I think they look more organic if they are slightly uneven and not perfect.) You can make the flowers as small or as large as you like. Refer to Flowers for the Tree, Steps 1–3 (page 37).

Add All the Shapes to the Background

To arrange all of the appliqué pieces on the background, it is helpful to use a design wall (page 8). If you don't have access to one, you can use a table or even the floor. Use the project photo (page 39) as a guide for placement. Refer to the stitching illustrations (page 9) as needed.

1. Arrange the flowers and leaves on the background, moving them around until you are happy with the color placement.

2. Pin the flowers and leaves in place with appliqué pins.

3. Arrange the stems so they come from the flowers to the top of the clamshell border. Cut the stems to size and, if necessary, clip the tacking on the clamshells to allow the stems to tuck underneath. Try to keep the stems curved in nice, soft lines. The curved lines add movement and interest to the overall composition. Note that not all of the flowers need to have stems; leave some floating around. When you are happy with the stem placement, pin them in place.

4. Add some more leaves to complete the design.

5. Appliqué the flowers in place with a backstitch and a variety of colors of perle cotton thread.

6. Stitch the stems in place with small running stitches in green perle cotton thread.

7. Stitch the leaves in place with small whipstitches in green perle cotton thread.

8. Finish stitching the top row of clamshells to the background.

9. Trim the center to straighten up the edges. The center piece should measure 42½″ × 13½″, including seam allowances.

Add the Borders

Seam allowances are ¼″.

Border 1

1. Stitch the 1½″ × 42½″ Border 1 strips to the top and bottom of the runner. Press the seams toward the border.

2. Stitch the 1½″ × 15½″ Border 1 strips to the sides of the runner. Press the seams toward the border.

Border 2

1. Randomly stitch the bright print 2″ × 3½″, 2½″ × 3½″, and 3″ × 3½″ Border 2 pieces together into a strip at least 132″ long. Press the seams.

2. Cut the long pieced strip to yield 2 strips 3½″ × 50½″ for the top and bottom and 2 strips 3½″ × 15½″ for the sides.

3. Stitch a 3½″ × 15½″ strip to each side, pressing the seams toward Border 1. Stitch the 3½″ × 50½″ strips to the top and bottom and press the seams toward Border 1.

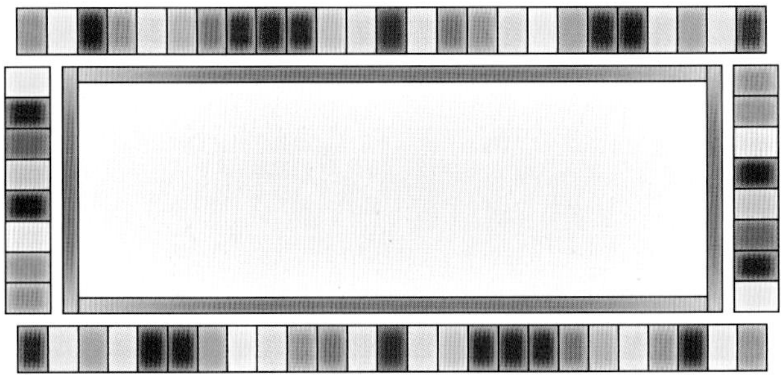

Quilt assembly diagram

Finish

1. Layer, baste, and quilt as desired. I hand quilted with perle cotton thread, outlining all of the flowers and stems. I also hand quilted all of the straight seamlines. Then I machine-quilted with small stippling stitches all over the cream background.

2. Use your preferred method to bind the edges.

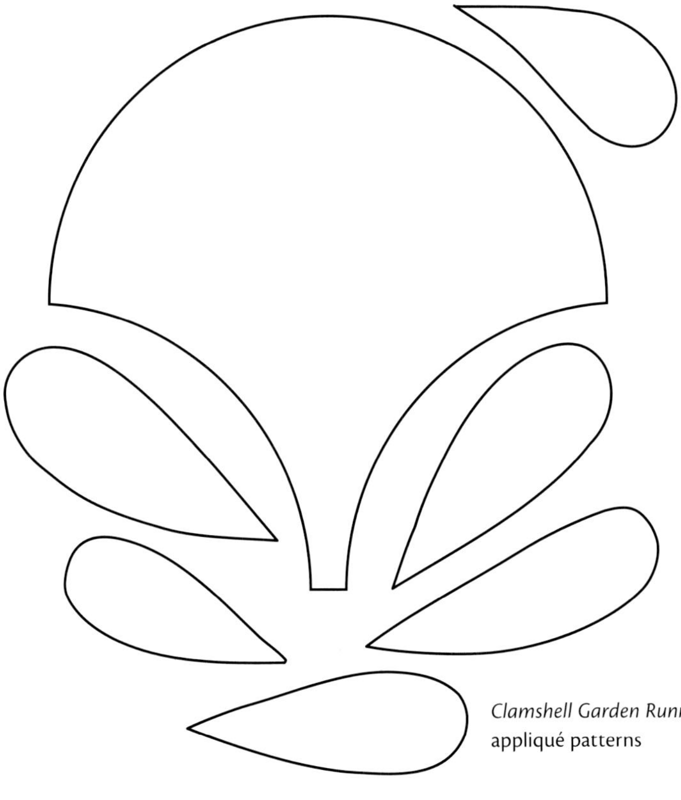

Clamshell Garden Runner appliqué patterns

Lovebird Pillows

Finished sizes: Owls: 19″ × 18½″ (48cm × 47cm) | Lovebirds: 20½″ × 17″ (52cm × 43cm)

These pillows are made from leftover pieces of printed linens. The linen background gives the pillows a simple contemporary feel. They are a great starting point for beginners, as the appliqué designs are quite simple and quick to achieve. Try mixing up the background with your leftover linen fabrics; you can also use cotton fabrics with small or large tone-on-tone prints.

The appliqué for the tree uses fusible web and is stitched by machine. All the other appliqué is done by hand.

MATERIALS

Yardage is based on 44″ (112cm) wide fabric, unless otherwise noted. Yardage and supplies are for only one pillow.

Linen or cotton: ¾ yard (70cm) total of assorted linen or cotton (This can be pieced with large scraps.)

Muslin (or similar): ¾ yard (70cm) for appliquéd pillow front backing

Fusible batting: 24″ × 24″ (61cm × 61cm)

Pillow form: 22″ × 22″ (56cm × 56cm) (I used the same size for both pillows but removed stuffing as needed.)

Paper-backed 20″ fusible web: ¾ yard (70cm)

Perle cotton thread: size 8 in a variety of colors, including black

Zipper: 16″ (40cm)

Owls pillow

Black cotton: ½ yard (50cm) for tree

Variety of wool felt: 5 squares 5″ × 5″ (15cm × 15cm) of purple, pink, mauve, blue-mauve, and plum

Black wool felt: 1 square 3″ × 3″ (7cm × 7cm)

Circle fabric print for eyes: 4 circles

Lovebirds pillow

Black wool felt: 1 square 10″ × 10″ (25cm × 25cm)

Black iron-on bias tape: ¼″-wide ¾ yard (70cm)

CUTTING

Seam allowances are ¼″ unless otherwise noted.

Linen or cotton

Owls

Pillow front: Cut 1 piece 19″ × 19½″, or cut fabric as shown. Stitch together the pieces as shown to make a rectangle 17½″ × 21″. *

Pillow back: Cut 2 pieces 10⅝″ × 19½″.

Lovebirds

Pillow front: Cut 1 piece 17½″ × 21″, or cut fabric as shown. Stitch together the pieces as shown to make a rectangle 19½″ × 19″. *

Pillow back: Cut 2 pieces 9⅞″ × 21″.

** If you are using scraps, feel free to stitch them together any way that works for you.*

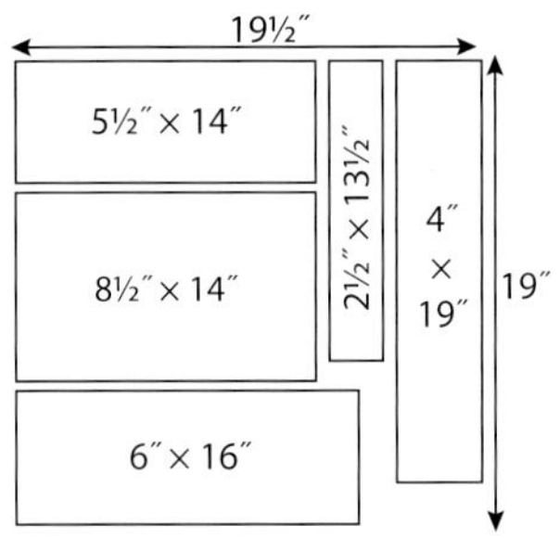

Owls pillow front: cutting and piecing from scraps

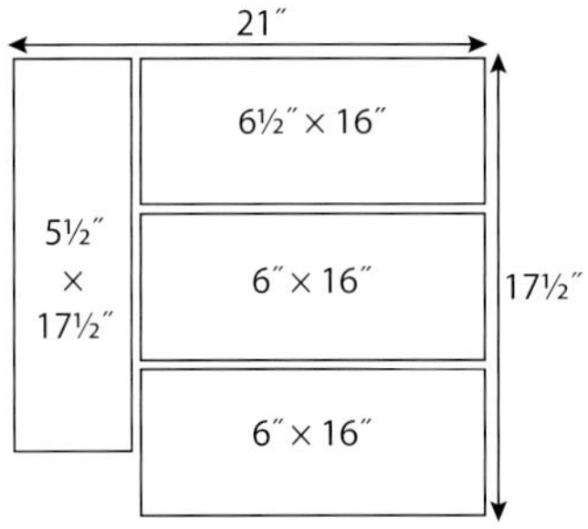

Lovebirds pillow front: cutting and piecing from scraps

Muslin and fusible batting

For the owls, cut 1 piece each 19″ × 19½″.

For the lovebirds, cut 1 piece each 17½″ × 21″.

Appliqué pieces

Copy the Lovebird Pillows *appliqué patterns (pullout page P2) at 100%. The patterns give you the shapes to cut, and the pattern pieces show suggested stitching.*

Owls tree

1. Trace the tree pattern onto the paper side of paper-backed fusible web. Cut out the tree, leaving a rough 1″ margin.
2. Following the manufacturer's instructions, fuse the fusible web to the wrong side of the black tree fabric and cut out the tree on the drawn line.

All other appliqué

Note: *All of these pieces are cut from wool felt, so there is no need to trace around the pattern to leave a seam allowance.*

1. Trace the appliqué patterns onto the dull (paper) side of freezer paper and cut on the drawn lines.
2. Press the freezer-paper templates onto the wool felt.
3. Cut out all of the appliqué pieces. Refer as needed to Appliqué Basics (page 5) for specific information on suggested fabrics for the appliqué pieces.
4. Cut out 2 pairs of eyes.

Appliqué

Note: I like to stitch as much of the appliqué as I can before I apply it to the background. Refer to Appliqué Basics (page 5) and Embroidery Stitches (page 9) as needed.

Tree and Owls

1. Remove the paper backing from the tree and iron the tree onto the background. The tree will fit edge to edge on the background piece. Machine stitch the tree in place with matching thread and a small zigzag or blanket stitch.

2. Pin the owls together, overlapping the wings ½″ over the body. Stitch by hand with perle cotton thread and a whipstitch.

3. Needle-turn the eyes onto the bodies.

4. Whipstitch the wings and noses onto the owls.

5. Position the owls on the tree and whipstitch in place.

Lovebirds and Wire

1. Press the bias tape in place on the pillow top, so the bias tape will be sewn into the seam allowance on each side of the pillow. Machine stitch the tape in place, stitching close to the edge on either side of the tape.

2. Pin the birds in place on the tape and stitch by hand with black perle cotton thread and a whipstitch.

Make the Pillow Front

1. Trim the pillow top according to the project instructions (owls: 19½″ × 19″; lovebirds: 21″ × 17½″), if necessary.

2. Press the fusible batting to the back side of the pillow front, following the manufacturer's instructions. Press lightly, as you don't want to flatten the felt shapes.

3. Place the muslin piece against the batting side of the front, and staystitch around the outside edges. This helps stabilize the appliqué and neaten the back of the pillow top.

Make the Pillow Back

Insert the Zipper

1. Use machine zigzag or overlock to neaten the long edges of the pieces where the zipper will be inserted. Then press under a 1″ seam allowance on each piece for the zipper. (For the owls pillow, the zipper will be inserted on the 19½″ length. For the lovebirds pillow, the zipper will be inserted on the 21″ length.)

2. Pin the zipper to one side of the pillow back so the folded edge is resting close to the zipper teeth. The zipper should be centered within the width of the piece.

3. With a zipper foot on the sewing machine, stitch close to the folded edge through the zipper tape. Start with the zipper open and stitch for approximately 4″. Stop with the needle down. Lift the presser foot and close the zipper. Then lower the presser foot and continue stitching to the end of the zipper tape.

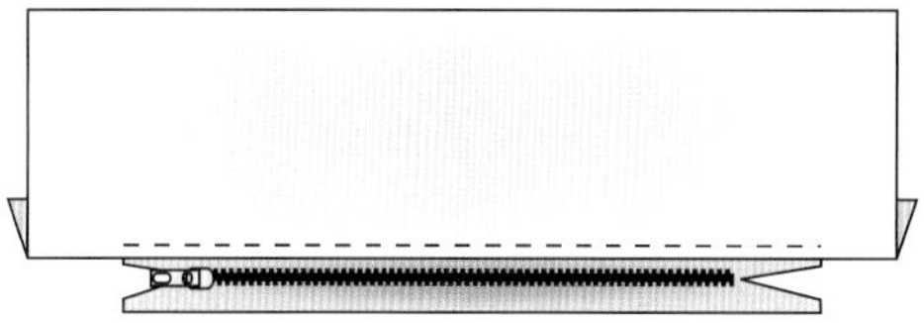

Fold and stitch first side of zipper.

4. Place the other side of the pillow back over the zipper, overlapping the folded edges approximately ⅛″. Pin along the folded edges.

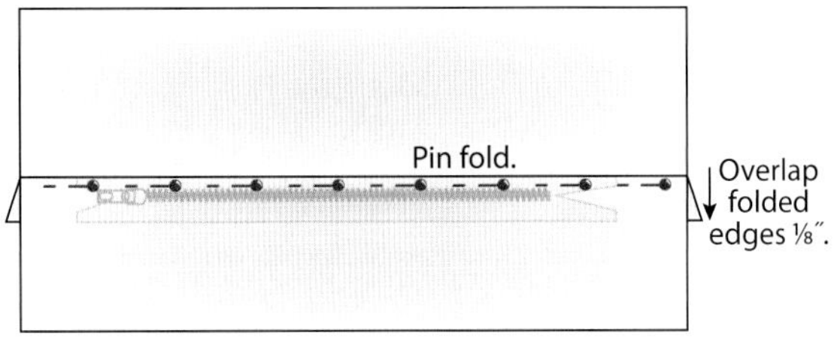

5. Mark each end of the zipper with a pin perpendicular to the folded edge, making sure the pins clear both ends of the zipper. Pin along the zipper about ½″ from the folded edge, making sure to pin through the zipper tape as shown.

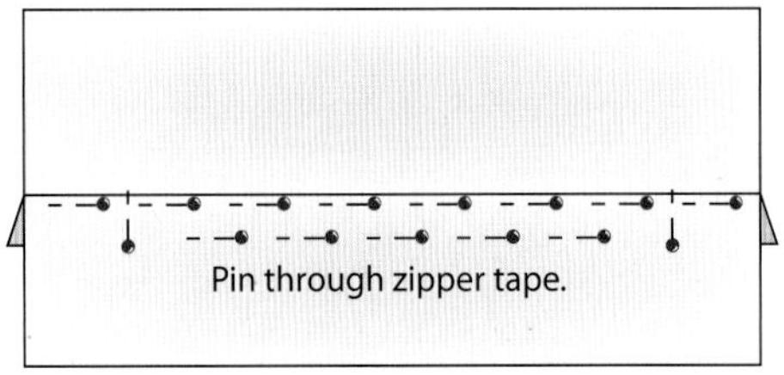

Pin ends of zipper and ½″ from fold.

6. Take out the first row of pins, leaving the pins that are attached to the zipper tape.

7. Open the zipper and using the zipper foot on the sewing machine, stitch along the edge until you reach the first perpendicular pin. Stop with the needle down, remove the pin, pivot, and stitch across the end of the zipper. With the needle down, pivot again and follow the pins to stitch the length of the zipper. Remove the pins as you stitch and close the zipper before you get to the end. When you reach the second perpendicular pin, pivot again with the needle down and stitch across the end of the zipper. Then pivot again and stitch along the fold.

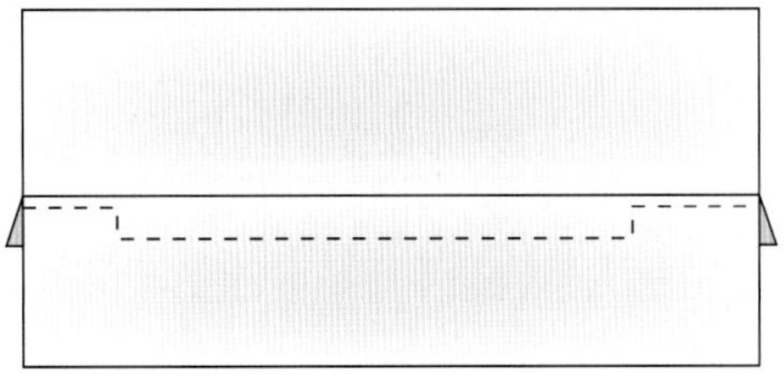

Stitch.

Finish the Pillow

1. Close the zipper *almost*, but not quite all the way, and place the pillow front and back right sides together. Trim the back to match the size of the pillow front.

2. Pin the pillow front and back together as shown. With the pillow front on top, mark a point with chalk or pencil approximately 1″ diagonally in from each corner. Pin around the pillow, keeping the edges together. Keep a ¼″ seam allowance at the sides, but gradually taper the pins in to the points marked on each corner. This will eliminate the dog ears on the completed pillow.

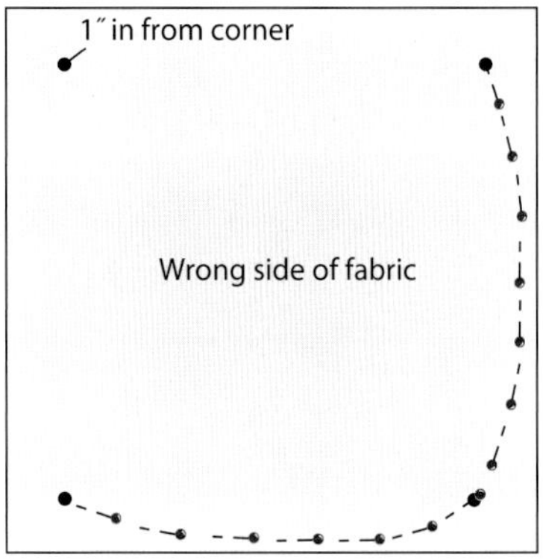

Mark 1″ from corner and pin around edges.

3. Stitch around the edge, pivoting at each corner with the needle down.

4. Finish the raw edges with a zigzag or overlock stitch.

5. Open the zipper all the way, and turn the pillow through to the right side, folding in the corner seam allowances. *Don't trim the corner seam allowances*, as this would weaken the points. Leaving the corner seam allowances will also help to give the corner some substance.

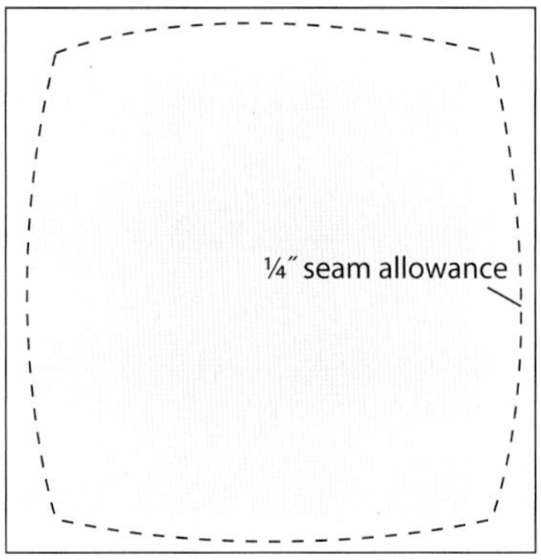

Stitch around pillow.

6. Insert the pillow form, removing the pillow stuffing as needed to fit the pillow you have made.

Still Life Pillows

Finished size: 20″ × 20″ (51cm × 51cm)

These pillows are fun to make. Use a variety of embroidery stitches and mix up the thread colors. You can use matching or contrasting colors. The background can be one piece of fabric, or it can be pieced to make a 20½″ × 20½″ square in any combination of fabrics and colors. This is a design where anything goes—just have fun!

MATERIALS

Yardage is based on 44″ (112cm) wide fabric, unless otherwise noted. Yardage is for 1 pillow.

Prints: ¾ yard (70cm) or several prints for piecing pillow front and back (I pieced mine with several different fabrics.)

Vase: 1 piece 6″ × 11″ (16cm × 30cm)

Bright wool felt: 8 pieces 5″ × 10″ (15cm × 25cm) in bright colors for flowers and bird

Green wool felt: 2 squares 10″ × 10″ (25cm × 25cm) of contrasting greens for stems and leaves

Black wool felt: 1 square 1″ × 1″ (2.5cm × 2.5cm) for bird's eye

Fusible batting: 20½″ × 20½″ (52cm × 52cm)

Muslin (or similar): ¾ yard (70cm) for appliquéd pillow top backing

Zipper: 18″ (46cm)

Perle cotton thread: size 8 in a variety of colors

Pillow form: 22″ × 22″ (56cm × 56cm)

CUTTING

Prints

Cut 1 square 20½″ × 20½″, or if you are piecing the pillow front, stitch the fabrics together and then cut the square.

Muslin

Cut 1 square 20½″ × 20½″.

Backing

Cut 2 pieces 11⅜″ × 20½″.

Appliqué pieces

Copy the Still Life Pillows *appliqué patterns (pages 107 and 108) at 100%. The patterns give you the shapes to cut, and the pattern pieces show suggested stitching. I don't always specify the exact number of pieces to cut, as this is your opportunity to make the project your own.*

Note: *For cotton or linen fabrics, trace around the freezer paper and cut out with a ¼″ seam allowance. For wool felt, there is no need to trace around the pattern or leave a seam allowance.*

1. Trace the appliqué patterns onto the dull (paper) side of freezer paper and cut on the drawn lines.

2. Press the freezer-paper templates onto the right side of the appropriate felt or fabric.

3. Cut out all the appliqué pieces. Refer as needed to the following suggestions for fabric for the appliqué pieces:

Vase: Use the appropriate template for the vase shape you want to use.

Green felt: Cut 10 leaves. Use a rotary cutter to cut stem strips approximately 1/4″ × 12″.

Felt for the bird: Use the appropriate templates for the bird shapes you want to use.

Bright felts: Cut small circles for the flower centers either using the templates or cutting them freehand.

Appliqué

Note: *I like to stitch as much of the appliqué as I can before I apply it to the background. Refer to Appliqué Basics (page 5) and Embroidery Stitches (page 9) as needed.*

Vase

Pin the vase to the background. Needle-turn the sides, leaving the top edge open to insert the stems.

Bird

Stitch the wing to the body using backstitch; then stitch the eye to the body with a colonial knot.

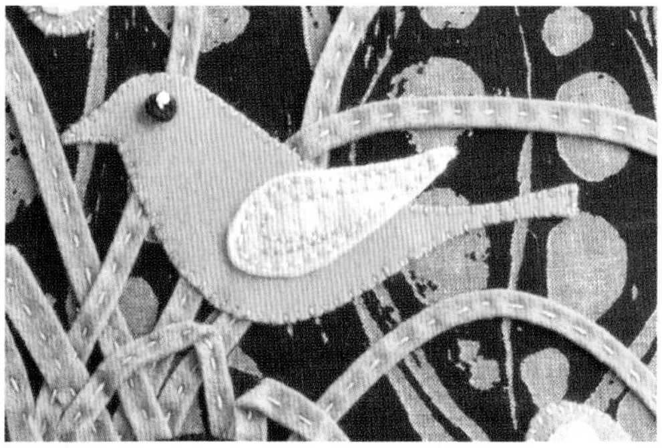

Flowers

1. On the smaller center circles, cut away a tiny circle in the center—this works like reverse appliqué, revealing the color of the background.

2. Refer to Flowers for the Tree (page 37) to stitch the flower centers to a larger piece of felt in a contrasting or complementary color. Follow the stitches indicated on the patterns or make up your own. After you have stitched the centers, cut out the larger circle. You can use the pattern as a guide or simply cut freehand.

Leaves

Stitch a small piece of the lighter green felt to the center of the leaves. Follow the stitches indicated on the pattern or make up your own.

Add All the Shapes to the Background

To arrange all of the appliqué pieces on the background, it is helpful to use a design wall (page 8). If you don't have access to one, you can use a table or even the floor. Use the project photo (page 47) as a guide for placement.

1. Arrange the flowers on the pillow front 20½″ × 20½″ background. Place the stems so that they start inside the vase and trail out to the flowers. The stems should extend approximately ½″ under the flowers. Arrange the leaves and the bird until you are happy with the composition.

2. Take a photo of your design that shows where all the pieces will go. Then take away the flowers, leaves, and bird and pin the stems to the background. Stitch the stems in place with running stitch or backstitch.

3. Place the flowers back on the stems; then pin and stitch them in place. Continue adding pieces, pinning and stitching as you go.

4. When you have completed the entire appliqué, stitch down the top edge of the vase.

5. You can add extra embellishment, such as buttons and beads, for added dimension.

Finish

1. Press the fusible batting to the back side of the pillow front, following the manufacturer's instructions. Press lightly, as you don't want to flatten the felt shapes.

2. Trim the pillow top if necessary. Place the muslin 20½″ × 20½″ piece against the batting side of the front, and staystitch around the outside edges. This helps stabilize the appliqué and neaten the back of the pillow top.

3. Refer to Pillow Back (page 45) and Finish the Pillow (page 46). Using the backing 20½″ × 11¼″ pieces, insert the zipper and finish the pillow.

Wee Farm Village Pillow

Finished size: 17″ × 25″ (43cm × 64cm)

On the south coast of New South Wales, about three hours from Sydney, there is a little town called Milton. I have a beach house near there, and when we go to the village to shop, I am always amazed by how green and lush the countryside is, even when the rest of the country is in drought. When you drive into town and come over the hill, you are hit with beautiful little farms with sheep and cows. At the top of the hill before you enter the village, there is a gorgeous little church. I always imagine that if I had a farm, this is where I would like it to be.

This pillow and the *Wee Village Town Pillow* (page 53) are my little pieces of Milton at my house in the city.

Wee Farm Village Pillow is made with all the little scraps of felt that I keep in a bag. It is complete with a wee barn, wee farmhouses, a wee church with a wee cemetery, and even a wee car. Wee sheep graze in the wee garden close to the wee houses. Wee trees offer some welcome shade from the hot summer sun.

The background for this pillow is linen, but it would work just as well with cotton or even fabrics with a wee print in tone-on-tone patterns. The appliqué houses are embellished before attaching them to the background. Use any of the embroidery stitches that you love. Play around with your color choices for the houses and stitching, using either matching or contrasting threads.

MATERIALS

Yardage is based on 44″ (112cm) wide fabric, unless otherwise noted.

Cream linen, 55″ (140cm) wide: ¾ yard (70cm) for pillow front and back

Muslin (or similar): ⅝ yard (35cm) for appliquéd pillow front backing

Wool felt: 10–12 squares 5″ × 5″ (15cm × 15cm) in a variety of colors, including white, brown, and green

Perle cotton thread: size 8 in a variety of colors

Zipper: 16″ (40cm)

Pillow form: 25½″ × 25½″ (65cm × 65cm) (I opened the pillow form and took out a little stuffing to make the pillow a rectangle.)

Batting: 21″ × 29″ (53cm × 74cm)

CUTTING

Linen

Cut 1 piece 17½″ × 25½″.

Cut 2 pieces 13⅞″ × 17½″.

Muslin

Cut 1 piece 21″ × 29″.

Appliqué pieces

Copy the Wee Farm Village Pillow *appliqué patterns (pullout page P1) at 100%. The patterns give you the shapes to cut, and the pattern pieces show suggested stitching.*

Note: *All of these pieces are cut from wool felt, so there is no need to trace around the pattern to leave a seam allowance.*

1. Trace the appliqué patterns onto the dull (paper) side of freezer paper and cut on the drawn lines.

2. Press the freezer-paper templates onto the right side of the appropriate felt or fabric.

3. Cut out all the appliqué pieces.

Appliqué

Note: *I like to stitch as much of the appliqué as I can before I apply it to the background. Refer to Appliqué Basics (page 5) and Embroidery Stitches (page 9) as needed.*

1. Stitch all of the windows, roofs, and so on to the appropriate pieces.

2. Mark a line for the base of the appliqué, approximately 10½″ down from the top edge of the linen 17½″ × 25½″ piece running across the pillow width. Stitch the line using green perle cotton thread and a running stitch.

Add All the Shapes to the Background

Using the project photo (page 50) and appliqué patterns (pullout page P1) as a guide for placement, start adding the shapes to the linen background 17½″ × 25½″ piece. Use appliqué pins to hold the shapes in place while you stitch them to the background. Add flowers using small dots of wool and colonial knots. You can add extra embellishment, such as buttons and beads, for added dimension.

Finish

1. Make a quilt sandwich, as you would for a quilt, using the appliquéd pillow front, batting, and muslin 21″ × 29″ piece for the backing.

2. Quilt as desired. I hand quilted the background with straight rows ¼″ apart below the appliqué, and some curved lines for the sky above the appliqué.

3. Trim the quilted pillow front to 17½″ × 25½″.

4. Refer to Pillow Back (page 45) and Finish the Pillow (page 46) to use the linen 13⅞″ × 17½″ pieces, insert the zipper, and finish the pillow.

Wee Village Town Pillow

Finished size: 20″ × 20″ (51cm × 51cm)

This is a companion to the *Wee Farm Village Pillow*. The background fabrics for this pillow are shot cotton in two shades of gray. Try using other colors or even small prints. Choose colors that allow the felt to contrast.

MATERIALS

Yardage is based on 44″ (112cm) wide fabric, unless otherwise noted.

Light gray shot cotton: ¾ yard (70cm) for pillow front

Dark gray shot cotton: 1 yard (1m) for pillow front and back

Muslin (or similar): ¾ yard (70cm) for backing the appliquéd pillow front

Wool felt: 8–10 squares 5″ × 5″ (13cm × 13cm) of different colors, including white

Black wool felt: 1 square 10″ × 10″ (25cm × 25cm)

Green wool felt: 2 squares each 10″ × 10″ (25cm × 25cm) of 2 different greens

Fusible batting: 20½″ × 20½″ (52cm × 52cm)

Zipper: 18″ (45cm)

Perle cotton thread: size 8 in a variety of colors, including black, white, and green

Pillow form: 22″ × 22″ (55cm × 55cm)

CUTTING

Light gray

Cut 1 square 20½″ × 20½″.

Cut 2 pieces 20½″ × 11¼″.

Dark gray

Cut 1 piece 10¼″ × 20½″.

Muslin

Cut 1 square 20½″ × 20½″.

Appliqué pieces

Copy the Wee Village Town Pillow *appliqué patterns (pullout page P1) at 100%. The patterns give you the shapes to cut, and the pattern pieces show suggested stitching.*

Note: *All of these pieces are cut from wool felt, so there is no need to trace around the pattern to leave a seam allowance.*

1. Trace the appliqué patterns onto the dull (paper) side of freezer paper and cut on the drawn lines.
2. Press the freezer-paper templates onto the wool felt.
3. Cut out all the appliqué pieces.

Appliqué

Note: *I like to stitch as much of the appliqué as I can before I apply it to the background. Refer to Appliqué Basics (page 5) and Embroidery Stitches (page 9) as needed.*

1. Stitch all of the windows, roofs, and so on to the appropriate pieces.

2. Pin the tree branches over the tree and whipstitch them in place.

3. Stitch the leaves to the tree with a backstitch.

Add All the Shapes to the Background

The curved dark gray fabric is appliquéd onto the light gray fabric.

1. To create the landscape curve, place the dark gray 10¼″ × 20½″ piece right side up on top of the right side of the light gray 20½″ × 20½″ square, keeping the lower edges even. With a chalk pencil, draw in a curved line on the dark gray piece, using the project photo (page 53) as a guide.

2. Trim the curve of the dark gray piece, leaving a ¼″ seam allowance. Pin and needle-turn the edge with a small running stitch close to the folded edge. Baste the outside raw edges of the gray fabrics together.

3. Using the project photo (page 53) and appliqué patterns (pullout page P1) as a guide, start adding the shapes to the background. Use appliqué pins to hold the shapes in place while you stitch them to the background. Add flowers using small dots of wool and colonial knots. Make the sheep faces with little chain stitches. Add apples to the tree with small colonial knots.

4. You can add extra embellishment, such as buttons and beads, for added dimension.

Finish

1. Fuse the fusible batting to the back side of the pillow front, following the manufacturer's instructions. Press lightly, as you don't want to flatten the felt shapes.

2. Place the muslin 20½″ × 20½″ piece against the batting side of the front, and staystitch around the outside edges. This helps stabilize the appliqué and neaten the back of the pillow top.

3. Refer to Pillow Back (page 45) and Finish the Pillow (page 46). Using the light gray 20½″ × 11¼″ pieces, insert the zipper and finish the pillow.

Wildflowers Bag

Finished size: 11″ × 13½″ (28cm × 35cm)

This simple little bag is a breeze to make. It is great for carrying magazines and books, and it also fits your tablet. The background fabric for this bag is wool. It would also work well with linen or even upholstery-weight fabric.

MATERIALS

Yardage is based on 44″ (112cm) wide fabric, unless otherwise noted.

Pink wool, 55″ (140cm) wide: ¾ yard (70cm) for body of bag

Medium green wool felt: 1 square 12″ × 12″ (31cm × 31cm) for leaves

Lime-green wool felt: 1 square 10″ × 10″ (26cm × 26cm) for leaves

Wool felt: 7 squares 4″ × 4″ (11cm × 11cm) in a variety of colors, including dark purple, blue, red, purple, orange, pink, and another green

Lining: ¾ yard (70cm)

Ribbon or flat trim: ½″–¾″ × 2¼ yards (1.3cm–2cm × 2m) for strap

Fusible batting: 15″ × 40″ (38cm × 102cm)

Perle cotton thread: size 8 in a variety of colors

Buckle: 1½″ wide (35mm)

2 D-rings: 1½″ wide (35mm)

Fusible nonwoven interfacing (*optional*): 2 squares 2″ × 2″ (5cm × 5cm)

Magnetic clasp (*optional*)

CUTTING

Pink wool

Cut 2 pieces 12″ × 14½″ for the bag front and back.

Cut 1 piece 2½″ × 39″ for the gusset.

Cut 1 piece 3¼″ × 49″ for the strap.

Cut 2 pieces 3¼″ × 10¼″ for the strap tabs.

Lining

Cut 2 pieces 12″ × 14½″ for the bag front and back.

Cut 1 piece 2½″ × 39″ for the gusset.

Batting

Cut 2 pieces 12″ × 14½″ for the bag front and back.

Cut 1 piece 2½″ × 39½″ for the gusset.

Appliqué pieces

Copy the Wildflowers Bag *appliqué patterns (page 109) at 100%. The patterns give you the shapes to cut, and the pattern pieces show suggested stitching.*

Note: *All of these pieces are cut from wool felt, so there is no need to trace around the pattern to leave a seam allowance.*

1. Trace the appliqué patterns onto the dull (paper) side of freezer paper and cut on the drawn lines.

2. Press the freezer-paper templates onto the wool felt.

3. Cut out all of the appliqué pieces. Refer as needed to the following suggestions for fabric for the appliqué pieces:

Green felt: Cut 2 strips ½″ wide in medium green and 1 strip 1″ wide in lime green for stems; then cut out the leaves.

Colored felt: Cut large circles using the freezer-paper templates and cut small circles freehand.

Appliqué

Note: *I like to stitch as much of the appliqué as I can before I apply it to the background. Refer to Appliqué Basics (page 5) and Embroidery Stitches (page 9) as needed.*

1. Whipstitch the small circles to the large circles. Use contrasting thread colors to add more interest to the design.

2. Stitch the centers to the leaves with a large whipstitch in a zigzag pattern.

Add All the Shapes to the Background

1. Use the project photo (page 56) as a guide for placing the shapes on the bag front 12″ × 14½″ piece. Arrange the appliqué pieces on the bag front and pin them in place, keeping in mind the ½″ seam allowance on all sides of the front. Stitch the appliqué in place with perle cotton thread.

2. Stitch the stems in place with a running stitch.

3. Stitch the flowers in place using a blanket stitch with the connecting stitches on the inside.

4. Scatter some small red dots on the background and stitch them with whipstitch in matching thread.

Make the Bag

Seam allowances are ½″ unless otherwise noted.

1. Press the appropriate fusible batting pieces to the wrong side of the appliquéd front, the wool back, and the wool gusset, following the manufacturer's instructions. Press lightly, as you don't want to flatten the felt shapes.

2. Mark the wool and lining gusset pieces as shown. Clip both sides of the gusset pieces 14″ from the cut edge on both ends and on both sides. Be careful not to clip in more than ½″, as this is the seam allowance of the gusset.

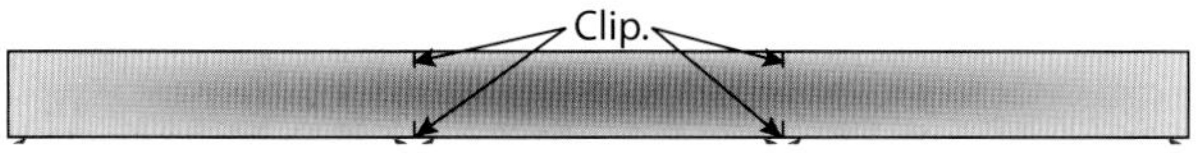

Clip gusset as marked.

3. Place the wool gusset on top of the appliquéd front, right sides together. Pin the gusset to the bag, matching the small clips to the corners. With the gusset side on top, stitch the pieces together. At each clip, put the needle down into the fabric, lift the foot, and pivot around the corner. You can go over the stitching at each corner to reinforce it.

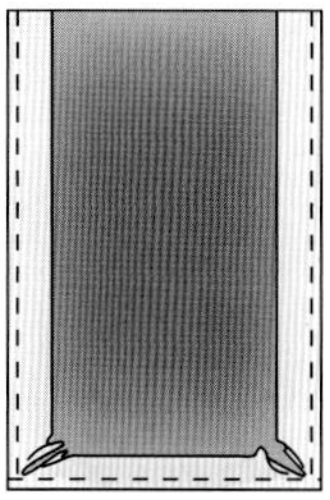

Pivot at corners.

4. Sew the bag back to the opposite side of the gusset, pinning, stitching, and pivoting as before. Turn the bag right side out.

5. Repeat Steps 2–4 using the lining front, back, and gusset pieces to make the lining. However, leave a 6″ opening along one side seam for turning the bag through to the right side later. (Do not turn the lining right side out yet.)

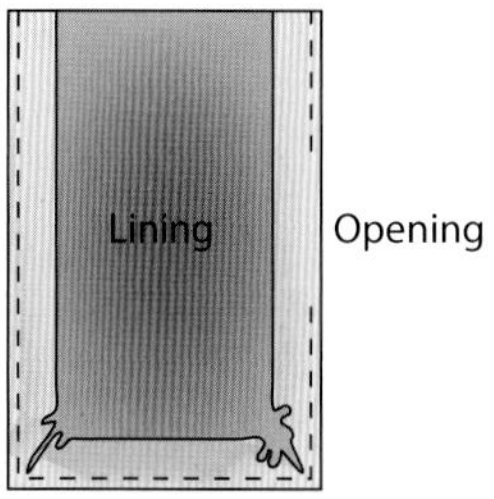

Leave 6″ opening.

Make the Straps

1. Press both wool 3¼″ × 10¼″ pieces and the wool 3¼″ × 49″ piece, folding the long edges into the center until they meet wrong sides together. Zigzag the edges together so that the zigzag stitch covers both raw edges.

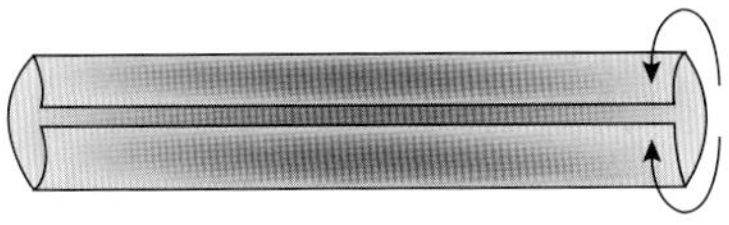

Fold edges to center.

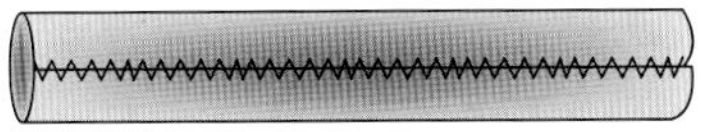

Zigzag edges together.

2. Center the trim over the long zigzagged raw edges of each strap and pin in place. Stitch the braid to the straps, stitching close to both edges of the braid. Zigzag the short ends of the straps to neaten.

Stitch trim over center zigzag and zigzag ends.

3. Thread a D-ring onto each 10¼″-long strap and fold the strap in half. Stitch 1″ from the fold, encasing the D-ring on each strap.

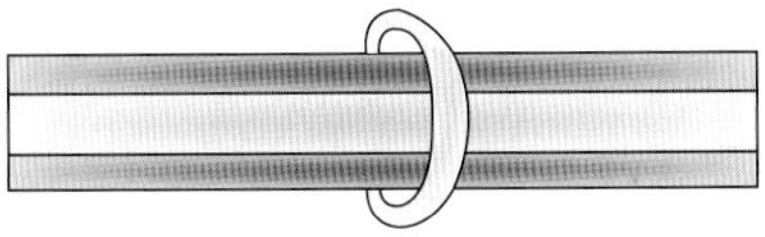

Thread D-ring onto each piece.

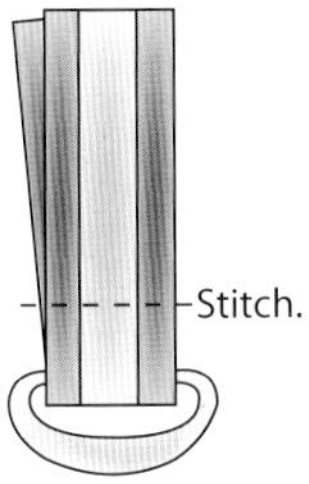

Fold and stitch 1″ from fold.

Assemble the Bag

1. Pin the small straps to the wool bag top, right sides together, approximately 1¼″ from the side seams. Make sure each strap goes from the front of the bag to the back of the bag (1 strap on each side) as shown. Stitch ½″ from the top edge to baste the straps in place.

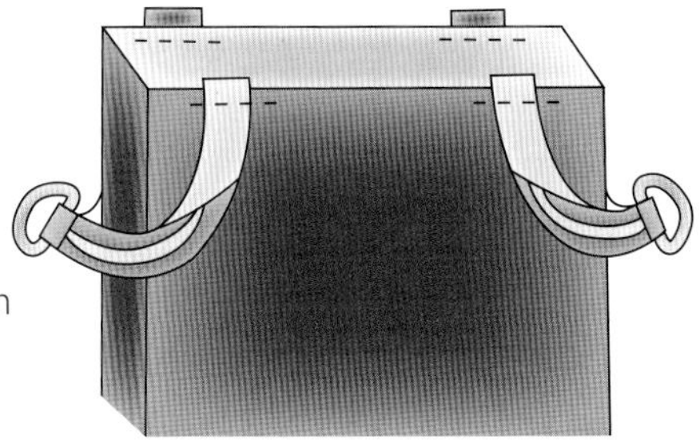

Pin and stitch straps to bag.

2. If you want to add a magnetic clasp to the bag, refer to *Bundles Bag*, Make the Bag, Step 9 (page 64).

3. Place the wool bag inside the lining bag, right sides together. Pin the lining to the bag around the top edges and then stitch together, catching the handles in place.

4. Turn the bag to the right side through the 6″ opening in the lining seam. Then stitch the opening in the lining closed.

5. Topstitch the width of the presser foot from the top edge of the bag.

6. Thread the long strap through the buckle and stitch down the end as shown.

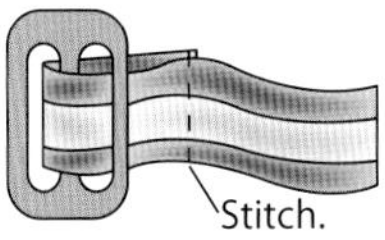

Stitch buckle in place.

7. With the wrong side of the strap facing up, pass the strap end (without the buckle) through one D-ring (A); then bring the end through the buckle (B). Pass the end through the other D-ring, keeping the braid to the outside. Pull the strap end up about 3″ and stitch it back on itself (C). You'll be able to adjust the strap to make it longer or shorter.

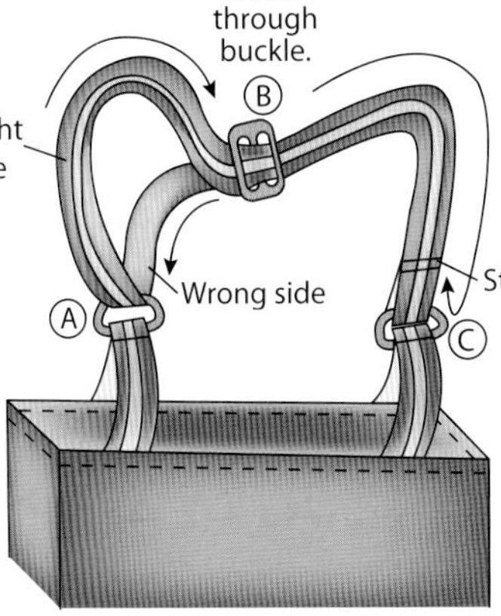

Thread strap through D-rings and buckle. Stitch.

Bundles Bag

Finished size: 13″ × 16″ (33cm × 40.5cm)

B*undles Bag* is a great bag to make and easy to wear. The strap is adjustable so that it can be worn over one shoulder or across the body. Make it in the colors shown or other combinations that suit your clothing style. My bag is made from wool, but it would work equally well in cotton or linen. Change the appliqué using some of the other patterns in the book for a completely different look. Looking at the project photo, you can see that I pieced the front of the bag with different colors of wool. If you have leftover pieces of wool from other projects, you might like to piece them together to make your own fabric to use. If you do, be sure to piece the colors together before cutting the bag pattern pieces.

MATERIALS

Yardage is based on 44″ (112cm) wide fabric, unless otherwise noted.

Red wool, 55″ (140cm) wide: ¾ yard (70cm) for bag front, back, gusset, and strap

Purple wool: 1 piece 7½″ × 11″ (19cm × 28cm) for front (A)

Mustard wool: 1 piece 6½″ × 11″ (16.5cm × 28cm) for front (B)

Lining: ¾ yard (70cm)

Dark green wool felt: 1 square 10″ × 10″ (25cm × 25cm) for tree

Medium and light green wool felt: 1 square 8″ × 8″ (21cm × 21cm) of each for leaves

Lime-green wool felt: 1 square 8″ × 8″ (21cm × 21cm) for leaves

Bright wool felt: 6″ × 6″ (16cm × 16cm) squares of 7 colors for flowers and dots

Black wool felt: 1 piece 2½″ × 6″ (6cm × 15cm) for tree trunk

Dotted print: 1 square 12″ × 12″ (31cm × 31cm) for flower centers

Fusible interfacing, such as Shape-Flex: 2 squares 2″ × 2″ (5cm × 5cm)

Perle cotton thread: size 8 in a variety of colors

Buckle: 1½″ wide (35mm)

2 D-rings: 1½″ wide (35mm)

Magnetic clasp

Ribbon or flat trim: ½″–¾″ × 2¼ yards (1.3cm–2cm × 2m) for strap

Appliqué pins

Fusible nonwoven interfacing *(optional)*: 1¼ yards (1.2m)

CUTTING

Copy the Bundles Bag *patterns for the bag front/back and the gusset (pullout pages P1 and P2) at 100%. The pattern pieces include the ¼″ seam allowance. Transfer indicated pattern markings to the fabric pieces.*

Red wool

Cut 1 piece 6½″ × 13½″ for the front (C).

Cut 1 bag front/back piece, using the pattern.

Cut 1 gusset piece using the pattern on fold. (The fabric can be pieced from red and purple to make up the length, as in the project photo on page 60.)

Cut 1 piece 3″ × 55″ for the strap.

Cut 2 pieces 3″ × 6″ for the strap tabs.

Lining

Cut 2 front/back bag pieces, using the pattern.

Cut 1 gusset piece using the pattern on fold.

Cut 1 square 4″ × 4″ for the pocket.

Appliqué pieces

Copy the Bundles Bag *appliqué patterns (pullout page P2) at 100%.*

Note: *For cotton or linen fabrics, trace around the freezer paper and cut out with a ¼″ seam allowance. For wool felt, there is no need to trace around the pattern or leave a seam allowance.*

1. Trace the appliqué patterns onto the dull (paper) side of freezer paper and cut on the drawn lines.

2. Press the freezer-paper templates onto the right side of the appropriate felt or fabric.

3. Cut out all the appliqué pieces. Refer as needed to the following suggestions for fabric for the appliqué pieces:

Dark green wool felt: Cut 1 treetop.

Black wool felt: Cut 1 tree trunk.

Green wool felts: Cut 15 leaves.

Dotted print: Cut 12 small circles, allowing a ¼″ seam allowance.

Make the Bag Front

Seam allowances are ¼″.

1. To make the bag front, sew the purple wool 7½″ × 11″ piece (A) to the mustard wool 6½″ × 11″ piece (B). Press the seam open. Then join the red wool 6½″ × 13½″ piece (C) as shown and press.

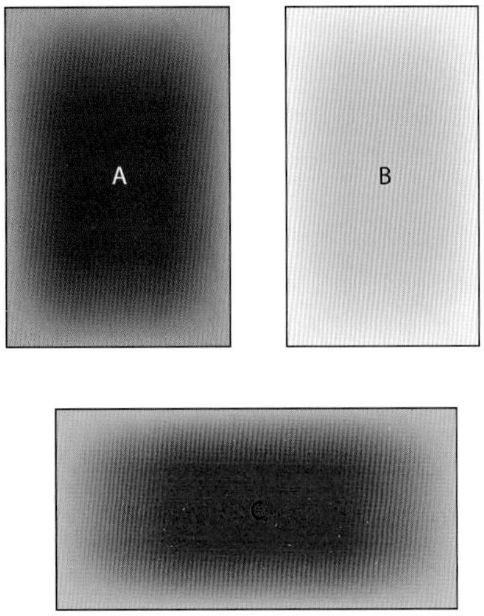

Piece bag front.

2. Cut out the bag front, using the front/back pattern piece. Align the pattern piece with the wool seamlines as indicated on the pattern.

Appliqué

Note: *I like to stitch as much of the appliqué as I can before I apply it to the background. Refer to Appliqué Basics (page 5) and Embroidery Stitches (page 9) as needed.*

1. Pin the tree and tree trunk to the bag front and stitch in place using perle cotton thread and a whipstitch, keeping in mind the ¼″ seam allowance around the outside edges of the front.

2. To make the circle flowers, refer to Flowers for the Tree, Steps 1–3 (page 37).

3. Scatter the circles on the tree and pin them in place. Stitch them to the tree with a running stitch.

4. Place the leaves on the tree and pin. Stitch them in place with a whipstitch.

5. Cut out some tiny dots from the scraps of felt and stitch them to the tree with small Xs.

Make the Bag

Seam allowances are ¼″.

1. Press the completed appliqué piece. This is optional, but I like to add fusible nonwoven interfacing to the wrong side of the appliquéd piece to give it more body. If you add interfacing, follow the manufacturer's instructions and press lightly, as you don't want to flatten the felt shapes.

2. Clip the seam allowance at the center of the appliquéd bag front and back at the lower edge. Place a small clip on either side of the center of the gusset as shown.

Clip bag front and back at center.

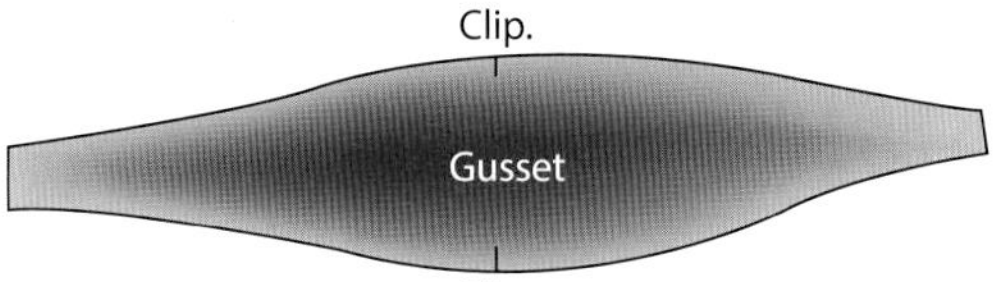

Clip on either side of center of gusset.

3. Pin and stitch the gusset to the front of the bag, easing around the corner and matching the clips. Stitch with the gusset side on top.

4. Repeat Step 3 to sew the bag back to the gusset. Turn the bag right side out.

5. Using the lining 4″ × 4″ square for the pocket, press a ¼″ seam allowance on all sides of the pocket piece to the wrong side.

Press pocket seam allowance to wrong side.

6. To form the pocket hem, turn down the pocket top 1″ to the wrong side and stitch along the folded edge as shown.

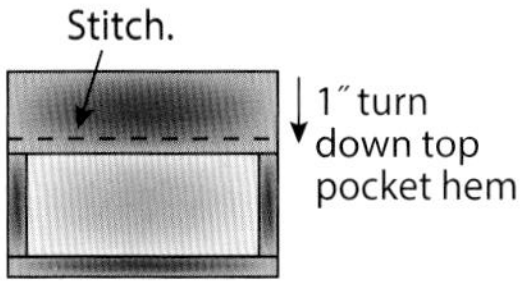

Turn down 1″ at top of pocket.

7. Match up the pocket corner on the right side of the back lining piece as indicated on the pattern and pin in place. Stitch the pocket to the lining.

8. Repeat Steps 2–4 using the lining pieces to form the lining for the bag, but leave an opening in one seam as indicated on the pattern. Do not turn the lining right side out yet.

9. On the lining front and back (centered and 2″ down from top edges), use a pencil to mark the position for the magnetic clasp as indicated on the pattern. Following the manufacturer's instructions, fuse a 2″ × 2″ square of fusible interfacing to the wrong side of the lining covering this position (A). Make 2 small clips as shown (B) and attach the clasp onto the right side of the lining (C).

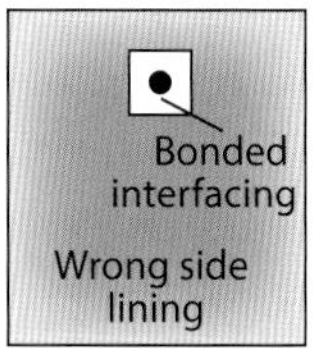

Fuse 2″ square of interfacing to wrong side of lining (A).

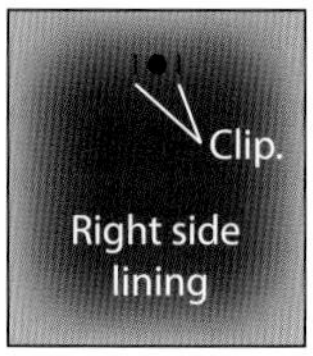

Clip lining (B).

Attach clasp to lining (C).

10. Place the wool bag inside the lining bag with right sides together. Pin the lining to the bag around the top edge and stitch the edges together.

11. Turn the bag to the right side through the opening in the lining seam. Stitch the opening in the lining closed. Then push the lining back inside the bag.

12. Topstitch the width of the presser foot from the top edge of the bag.

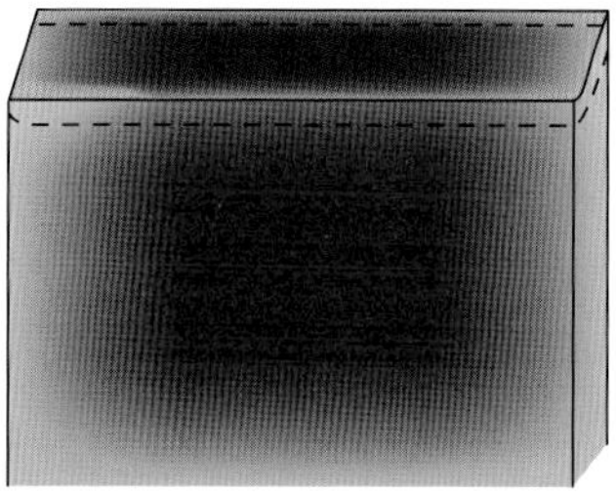

Topstitch around top edge.

Make the Straps

1. Press the red wool 3″ × 55″ piece and both red wool 3″ × 6″ pieces, folding the long edges into the center until they meet wrong sides together. Zigzag the edges together so that the zigzag stitch covers both raw edges.

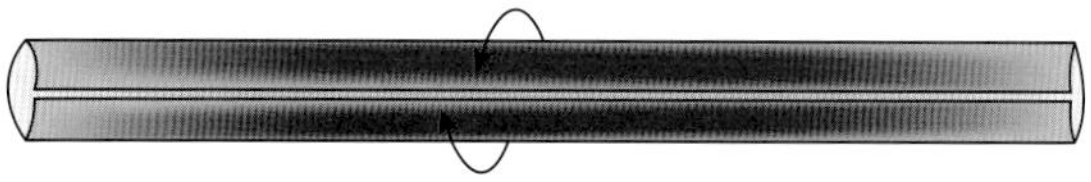

Press edges to center.

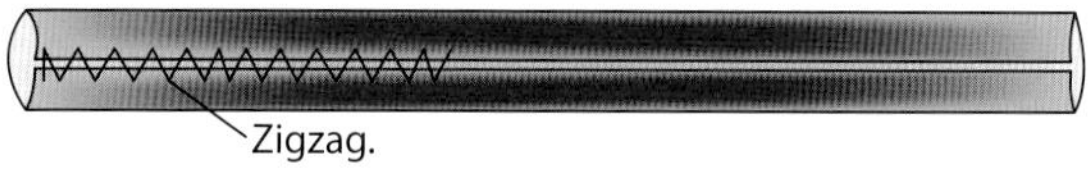

Zigzag edges.

2. Center the trim over the long zigzagged raw edges of each strap and pin in place. Stitch the trim to the straps, stitching close to both edges of the braid. Zigzag the short ends of the straps to neaten.

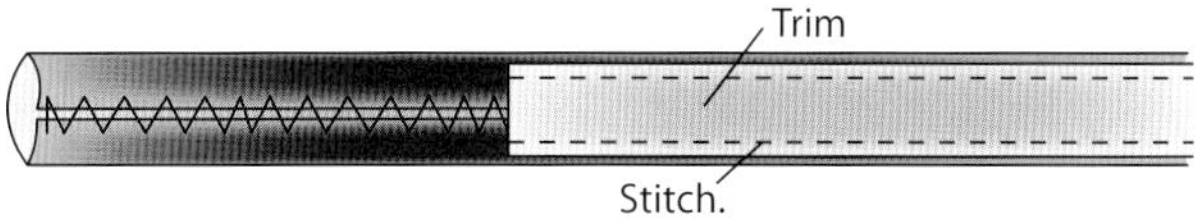

Stitch trim over zigzag.

3. With the trim against the right side of the gusset, position the end of a short strap on each side of the gusset as shown and as marked on the pattern. Using a ½″ seam allowance, stitch the small straps in place. Doublestitch to reinforce the strap.

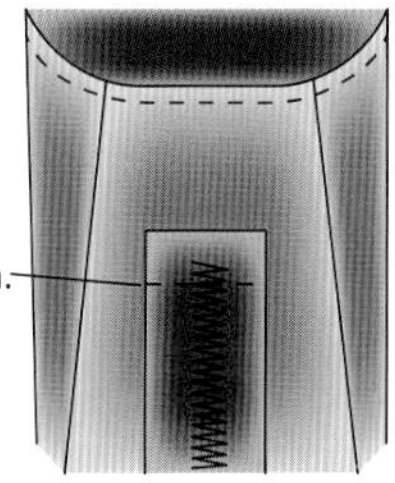

Stitch small strap pieces to gusset.

4. Fold up each small strap and stitch ¼″ from the fold as shown.

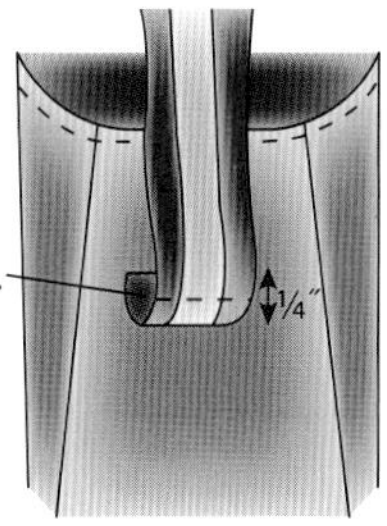

Fold strap up and stitch.

5. Thread the strap through the D-ring. Fold the strap against itself so the braid is on the outside and bring the raw edges of the strap together. From the outside of the bag, stitch ½″ above the secured end of the strap as shown, encasing the strap's raw edges. Slide the D-ring to the top of the folded strap and stitch the strap to the bag just below the D-ring. Repeat this step for the other side.

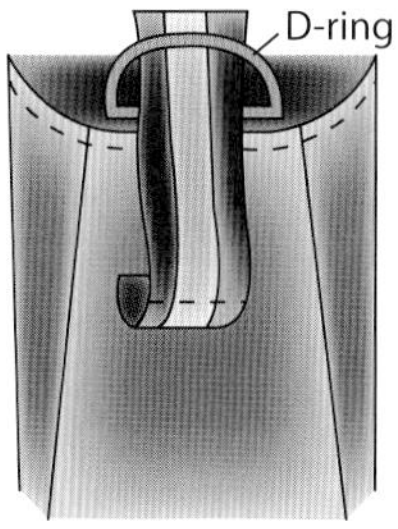

Thread D-ring on strap.

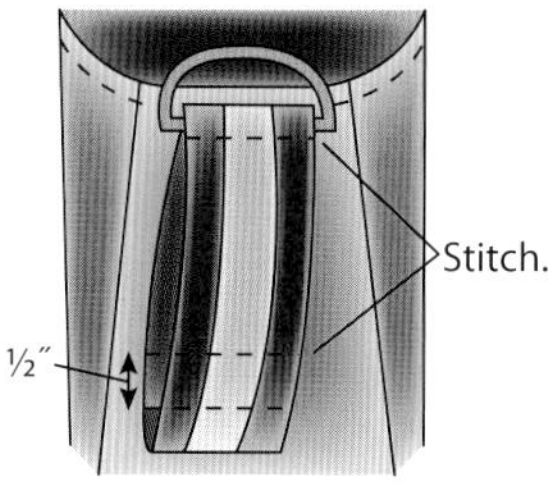

Stitch.

6. Thread the long strap through the center of the buckle and stitch the strap to itself as shown.

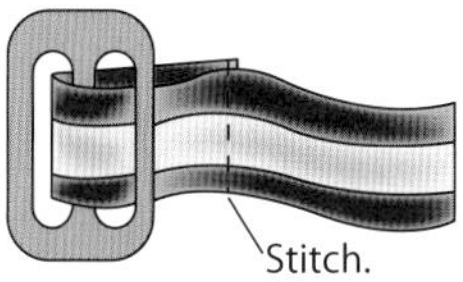

Stitch.

7. With the wrong side of the strap facing up, pass the strap end (without the buckle) through one D-ring (A); then bring the end through the buckle (B). Pass the end through the other D-ring, keeping the braid to the outside. Pull the strap end up about 3″ and stitch it back onto itself (C). You'll be able to adjust the strap to make it longer or shorter.

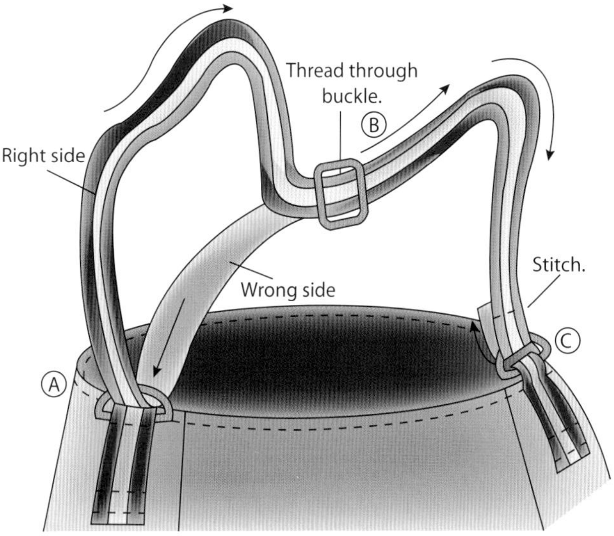

Thread strap through D-rings and buckle. Stitch.

Little Birds Sewing Kit

Finished size: 9″ × 5½″ (23cm × 14cm)

The size will vary depending on the ready-made sewing bag that you choose to embellish.

Front

Back

This little flock of birds resting on a branch is a great way to personalize any small project, like a sewing kit. Stitch some simple flowers and a branch of funky birds onto a piece of wool and simply attach it to your bag. You can adapt this project to suit your bag.

MATERIALS

Purchased sewing bag: Mine was 9″ × 5½″ × 2″ (23cm × 14cm × 5cm).

Wool: 1 square 12″ × 12″ (30cm × 30cm) for background *(Note: Adjust this size as needed to fit your purchased sewing bag.)*

Wool felt: 12 squares 5″ × 5″ (13cm × 13cm) in a variety of colors for birds, flowers, and leaves

Black wool felt: 1 piece 2″ × 8″ (5cm × 20cm) for branch, eyes, and beaks

White wool felt: 1 piece 2″ × 2″ (5cm × 5cm) for eyes

Dotted print: 3 circle motifs for flower centers

Perle cotton thread: size 8 or 10 in a variety of colors, including green and white

Ribbon, 1″ (2.5cm) wide: ½ yard (50cm) *(Note: Adjust this size as needed to fit your purchased sewing bag.)*

Ribbon, ½″ (12mm) wide: ½ yard (50cm)

CUTTING

Note: *Adjust sizes as needed to fit your purchased sewing bag.*

Background wool

Cut 1 piece 7″ × 10″ or to fit the front of your bag.

Cut 1 piece 5″ × 10″ or to fit the back of your bag.

Cut 1 piece 2½″ × 4½″ or to fit your handle length and wrap around handle.

½″-wide ribbon

Cut into 2 pieces 9″ long.

Appliqué pieces

Copy the Little Birds Sewing Kit *appliqué patterns (page 110) at 100%.*

Note: *For cotton or linen fabrics, trace around the freezer paper and cut out with a ¼″ seam allowance. For wool felt, there is no need to trace around the pattern or leave a seam allowance.*

1. Trace the appliqué patterns onto the dull (paper) side of freezer paper and cut on the drawn lines.

2. Press the freezer-paper templates onto the right side of the appropriate felt or fabric.

3. Cut out all the appliqué pieces. Refer as needed to the following suggestions for fabric for the appliqué pieces:

Colored felt: Cut out all the birds.

Green felt: Use a rotary cutter to cut strips 1¼″ × 2″; then cut the leaves.

Black felt: Cut 6 small circles for the birds' eyes, 2 beaks, and a ¼″-wide strip for the branch.

Dotted print: Cut 3 small circles, allowing a ¼″ seam allowance.

Appliqué

Note: *I like to stitch as much of the appliqué as I can before I apply it to the background. Refer to Appliqué Basics (page 5) and Embroidery Stitches (page 9) as needed.*

Front

1. Stitch all of the birds together, stitching on the wings with a running stitch.

2. Attach the beaks and eyes with tiny whipstitches.

3. Use white perle cotton thread to add a colonial knot to the centers of the birds' eyes.

4. Pin the wool background 7″ × 10″ piece (or the size piece you cut for the front) onto the front of the bag and mark the shape of the bag on the wool felt with a chalk pencil. Remove this piece before stitching the appliqué.

5. Pin the birds along the center of the background fabric. Use the project photo (page 66) as a guide for placement.

6. Stitch the birds in place using whipstitch and backstitch.

7. Place the branch across the lower parts of the birds. Pin and stitch down the branch using a whipstitch in black perle cotton thread.

8. Scatter the leaves to fill the background space and pin them in position. Stitch them in place with backstitch.

9. Stitch the birds' feet over the branch with long straight stitches.

Back

1. To make the circle flowers, refer to Flowers for the Tree (page 37).

2. Pin the wool background 5″ × 10″ piece (or the piece you cut for the back) onto the bag back and mark the shape of the bag with a chalk pencil. Remove this piece before stitching the appliqué to the back.

3. Stitch the 1″-wide ribbon to the top edge of the back piece, overlapping the ribbon ½″ over the edge of the wool fabric so the seam is flat.

4. Pin the stems, flowers, and leaves to the wool background and stitch them in place, stitching the stems with a backstitch, the leaves with a fly stitch, and the flowers with a running stitch.

Finish

1. Trim the front appliquéd piece that you marked, allowing a ½″ seam allowance all around.

2. Use flat-head pins to pin the front piece onto the front of the bag, turning under the seam as you go.

3. Stitch the front piece to the bag with a slip stitch and matching perle cotton thread. (It is helpful to do this with an upholstery needle and a thimble.)

4. Repeat Steps 1–3 for the back. The ribbon edge goes right up to the piping (of my premade bag). Slipstitch the ribbon to the piping.

5. Fold under ½″ on the 2 short ends of the 2¼″ × 4½″ wool piece. Wrap the piece around the handle and whipstitch the long edges closed along the top of the handle. Place a 1″-wide ribbon of braid over the seam, turning the raw edges under ½″. Pin to the wool. Whipstitch all around the ribbon.

6. Tie the ½″-wide ribbon pieces through the rings on the zipper pull.

Woolly Needle Case

Finished size: Open: 10″ × 8″ (25cm × 20cm) | Shut: 5″ × 8″ (15cm × 20cm)

Exterior

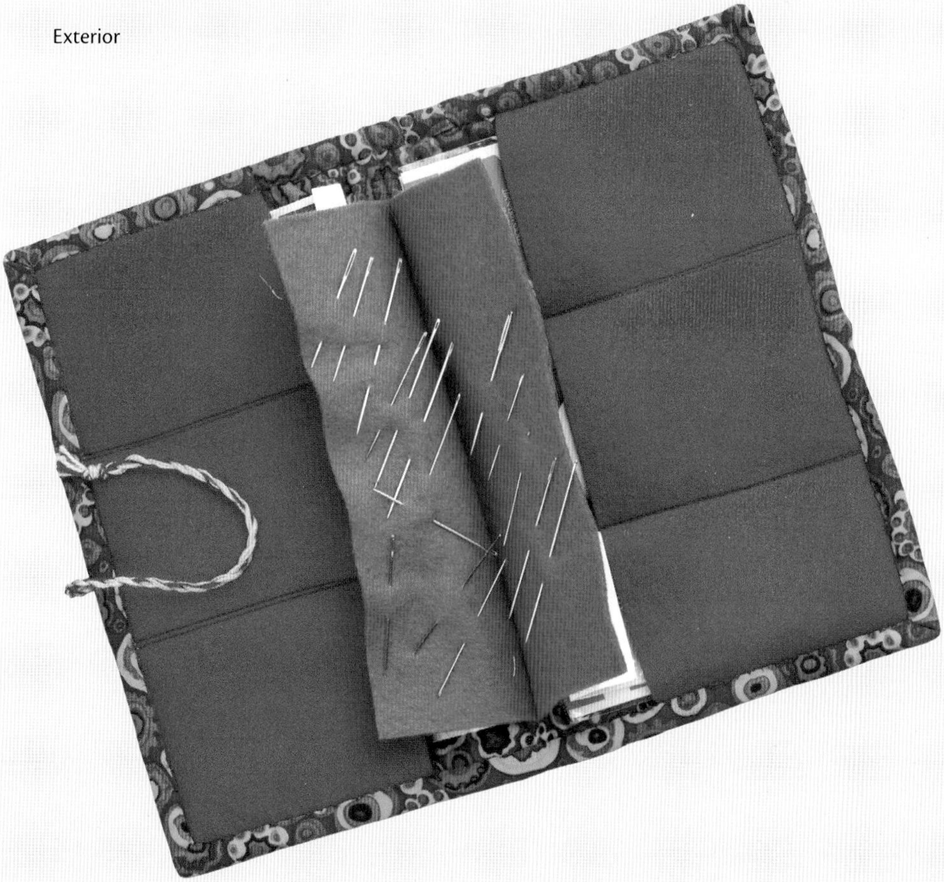

Interior

This little needle case not only looks great but is also really practical and easy to use. The pockets inside store all of your needles in their packets, and the folded sleeve is great for loose needles and pins.

Make this in your favorite colors and decorate with a little row of houses like mine or use some of the other designs in this book. Make more than one—they make great gifts for your stitching friends.

MATERIALS

Yardage is based on 44″ (112cm) wide fabric, unless otherwise noted.

Wool felt: 2 pieces 8″ × 10″ (20cm × 25cm) in different colors for exterior of case and interior pockets

Wool felt: 1 piece 4″ × 7″ (10cm × 18cm) of a coordinating color for center flap

Wool felt: 10 squares 4″ × 4″ (10cm × 10cm) in a variety of colors, including lime green

Cotton print: ¼ yard (23cm) for inside of case

Binding: ⅛ yard (11cm)

Fusible batting: 8″ × 10″ (20cm × 25cm)

Button: ½″ (12mm) diameter

Perle cotton thread: size 8 in a variety of colors

CUTTING

Wool felt

From an 8″ × 10″ piece, cut 2 pieces 3½″ × 8″ for the interior pockets.

Cotton print

Cut 1 piece 8″ × 10″.

Appliqué pieces

Copy the Woolly Needle Case *appliqué patterns (page 109) at 100%. The patterns give you the shapes to cut, and the pattern pieces show suggested stitching.*

Note: *All of these pieces are cut from wool felt, so there is no need to trace around the pattern to leave a seam allowance.*

1. Trace the appliqué patterns onto the dull (paper) side of freezer paper and cut on the drawn lines.

2. Press the freezer-paper templates onto the right side of the appropriate felt colors and cut around the templates (there is no need to leave a seam allowance).

3. Cut out all the appliqué pieces. Refer as needed to the following suggestions for fabric for the appliqué pieces:

Colored felt: Cut out all the buildings, roof pieces, chimneys, windows, and flowers.

Lime-green felt: Cut out a narrow, curving strip for the grass below the buildings.

Appliqué

Note: *I like to stitch as much of the appliqué as I can before I apply it to the background. Refer to Appliqué Basics (page 5) and Embroidery Stitches (page 9) as needed.*

1. Fold the exterior background wool felt 8″ × 10″ piece in half so the folded piece is 5″ × 8″. This creates the front appliqué area.

2. Using the project photo (page 69) and appliqué patterns (page 109) as a guide for placement, start adding the shapes to the background. Keep in mind that there is a ¼″ seam allowance along the raw edges. Use appliqué pins to hold the shapes in place while you stitch them to the background.

3. Appliqué all of the windows, doors, and roofs. Add flowers using small dots of wool and colonial knots. Stitch the stems with backstitch and the leaves with chain stitch.

TIP

You can add extra embellishment to the design if you wish. Beads and buttons will add extra dimension.

Make the Case

Seam allowances are ¼″.

1. Following the manufacturer's instructions, fuse the fusible batting to the wrong side of the print 8″ × 10″ piece.

2. Place the 2 wool felt 3½″ × 8″ pieces for the pockets onto the right side of the print fabric, aligning the 8″ outside edges. Draw chalk lines on the felt 2¾″ from each end as shown and stitch in place along these lines to create the pockets.

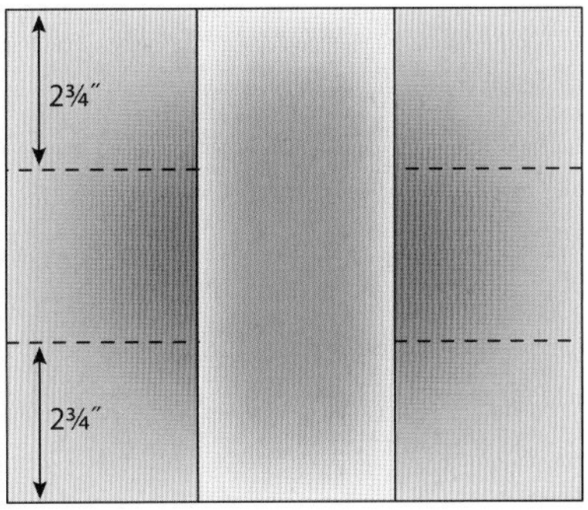

Mark and stitch pockets.

3. Pin the exterior appliquéd piece to the print piece so the batting is sandwiched between the wrong sides of the wool felt and the print piece. Stitch close to the outer edge all the way around the sandwich.

4. With wrong sides together, press the binding strip in half along the long edge, folding in the ends as you would for a quilt binding.

5. Attach the binding to the needle case as you would for a quilt binding, machine stitching onto the outside of the case and hand stitching along the inside edge.

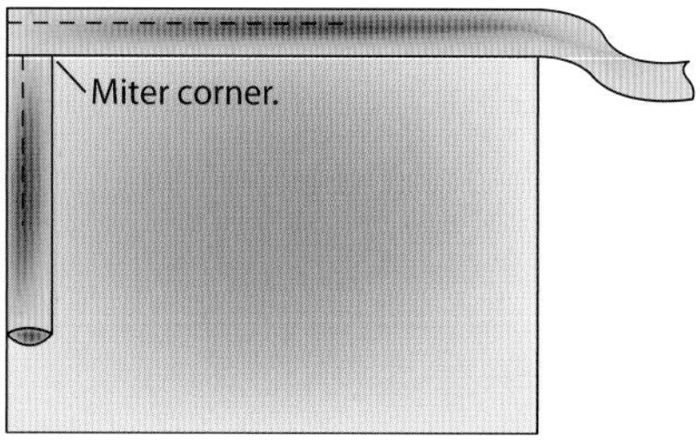

Attach binding.

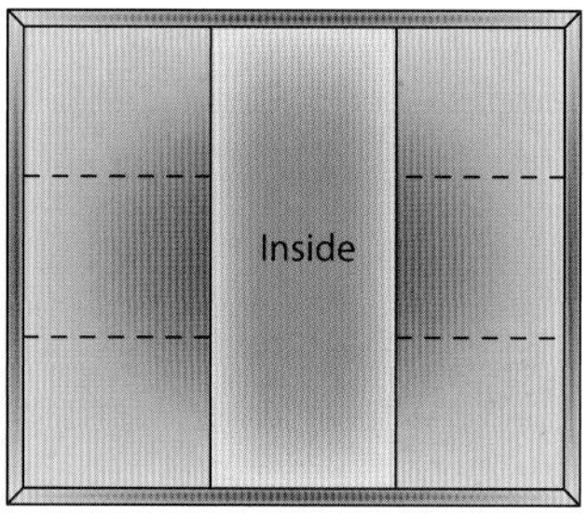

Fold to inside and hand stitch.

6. With the sewing kit open, center and pin the wool felt 4″ × 7″ piece onto the print fabric as shown. Stitch in place through the center length, stitching through all layers.

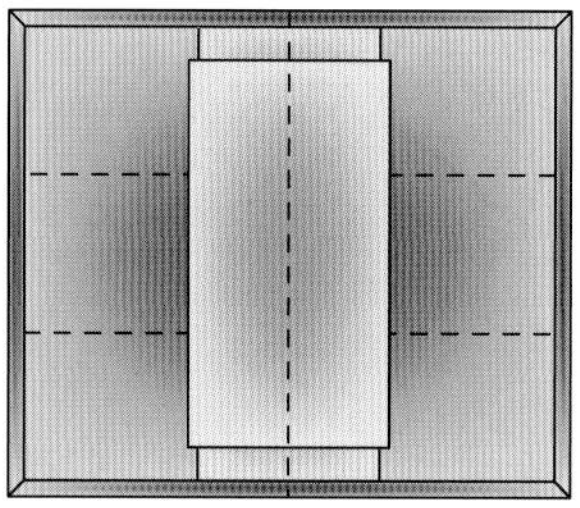
Add 4″ felt strip to center.

Make the Closure

1. Cut 2 lengths each 16″ long of perle cotton.

2. Secure to a door handle or have someone hold one end tight while you twist the threads together. When the threads start to twist and curl up on themselves, hold the twist in the center and release the 2 ends. This will allow the threads to twist together. Knot the end to prevent it from raveling.

3. Hand stitch the twisted cord to the front of the needle case along the binding seam. Stitch the button to the back of the needle case as shown. To close, simply twist the cord around the button.

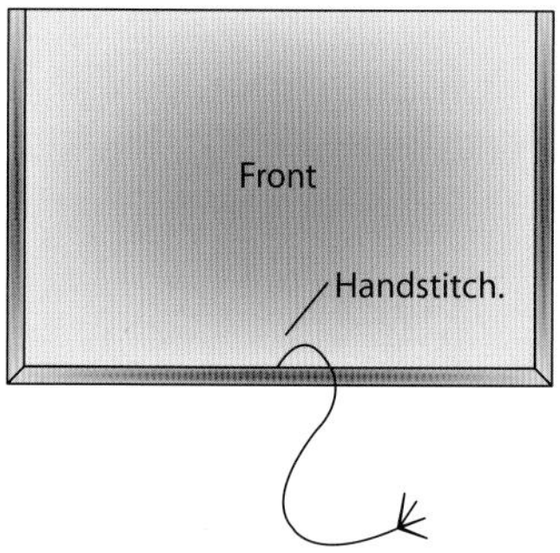

Hand stitch twisted cord to front.

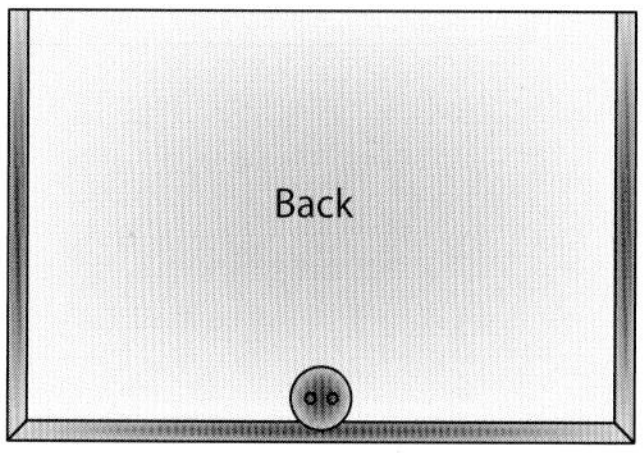

Stitch button to back.

Appliqué Patterns

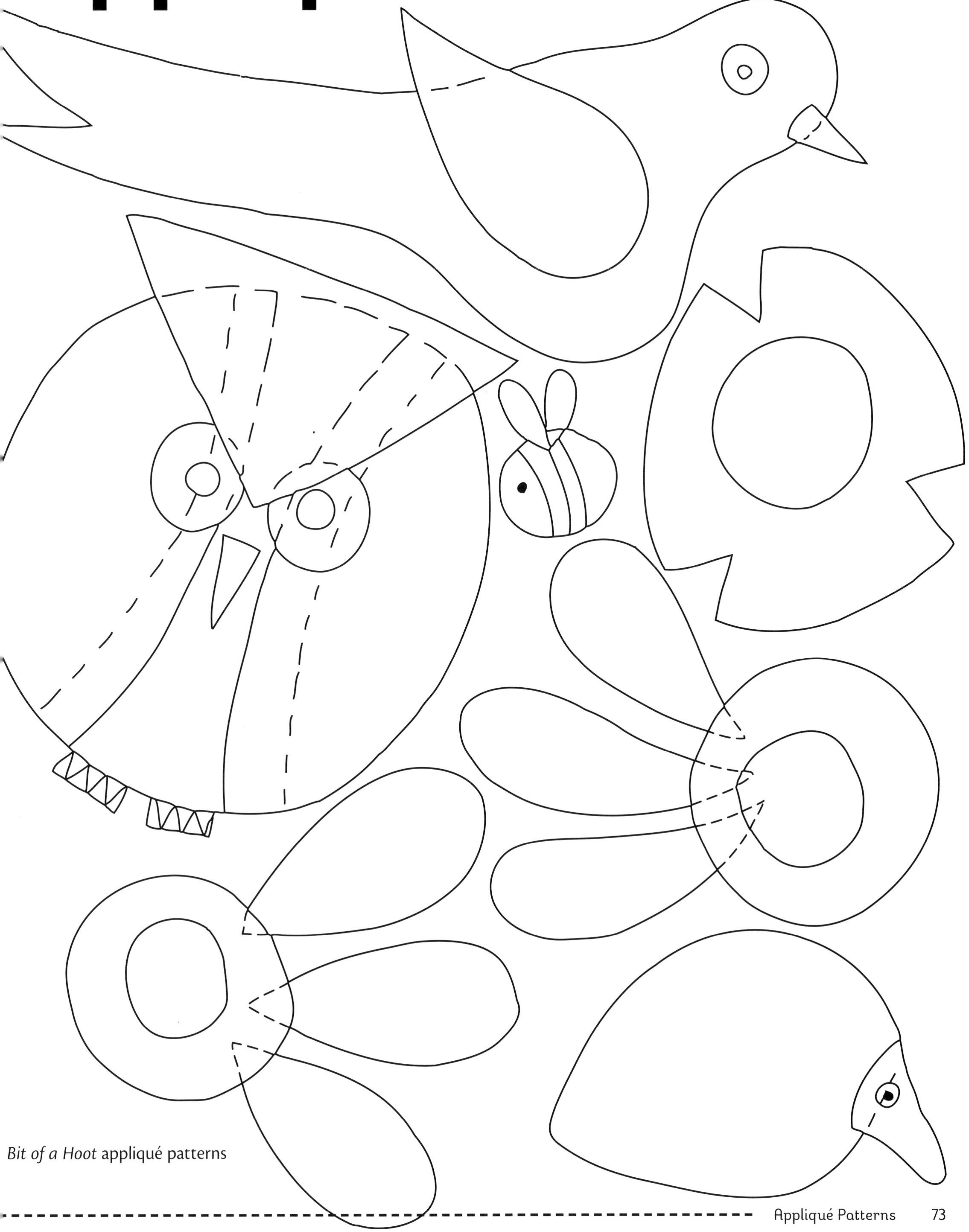

Bit of a Hoot appliqué patterns

A Bit of a Hoot appliqué patterns

A Bit of a Hoot appliqué patterns

Hooterville appliqué patterns

Hooterville appliqué patterns

Hooterville appliqué patterns

Hooterville appliqué patterns

Hooterville appliqué patterns

Hooterville appliqué patterns

Hooterville appliqué patterns

Hooterville appliqué patterns

Birds on a Wire appliqué patterns

Birds on a Wire appliqué patterns

Birds on a Wire appliqué patterns

Birds on a Wire appliqué patterns

Birds on a Wire
appliqué patterns

Two's Company
appliqué patterns

Two's Company appliqué patterns

Two's Company appliqué patterns

Two's Company
appliqué patterns

Two's Company appliqué patterns

Two's Company appliqué patterns

Two's Company appliqué patterns

Two's Company appliqué patterns

L=Light green
D=Dark green

Two's Company
appliqué patterns

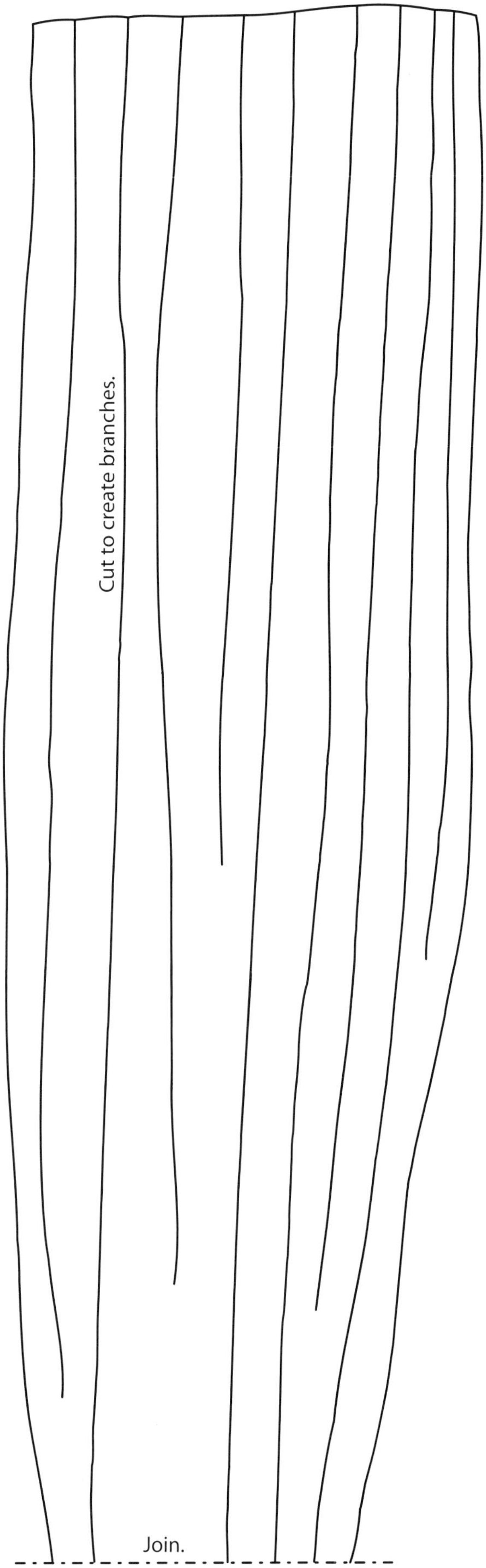

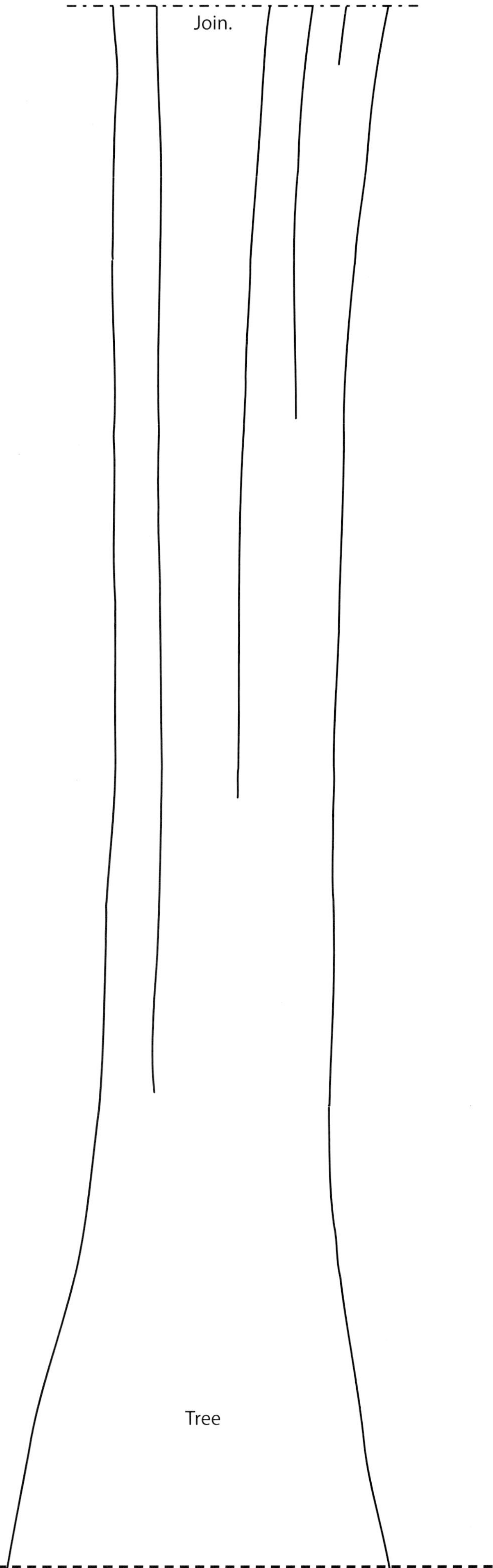

Two's Company appliqué patterns

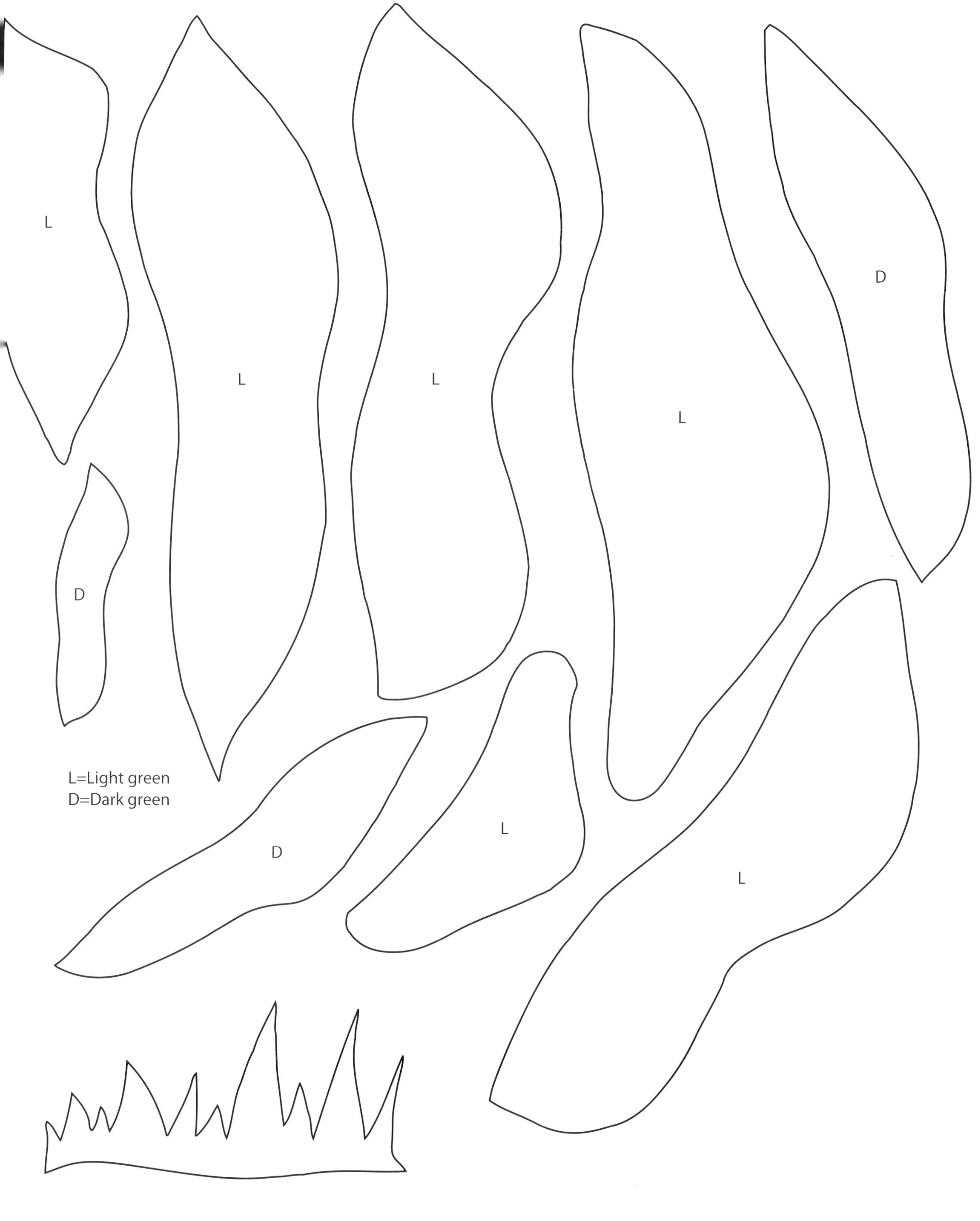

Two's Company appliqué patterns

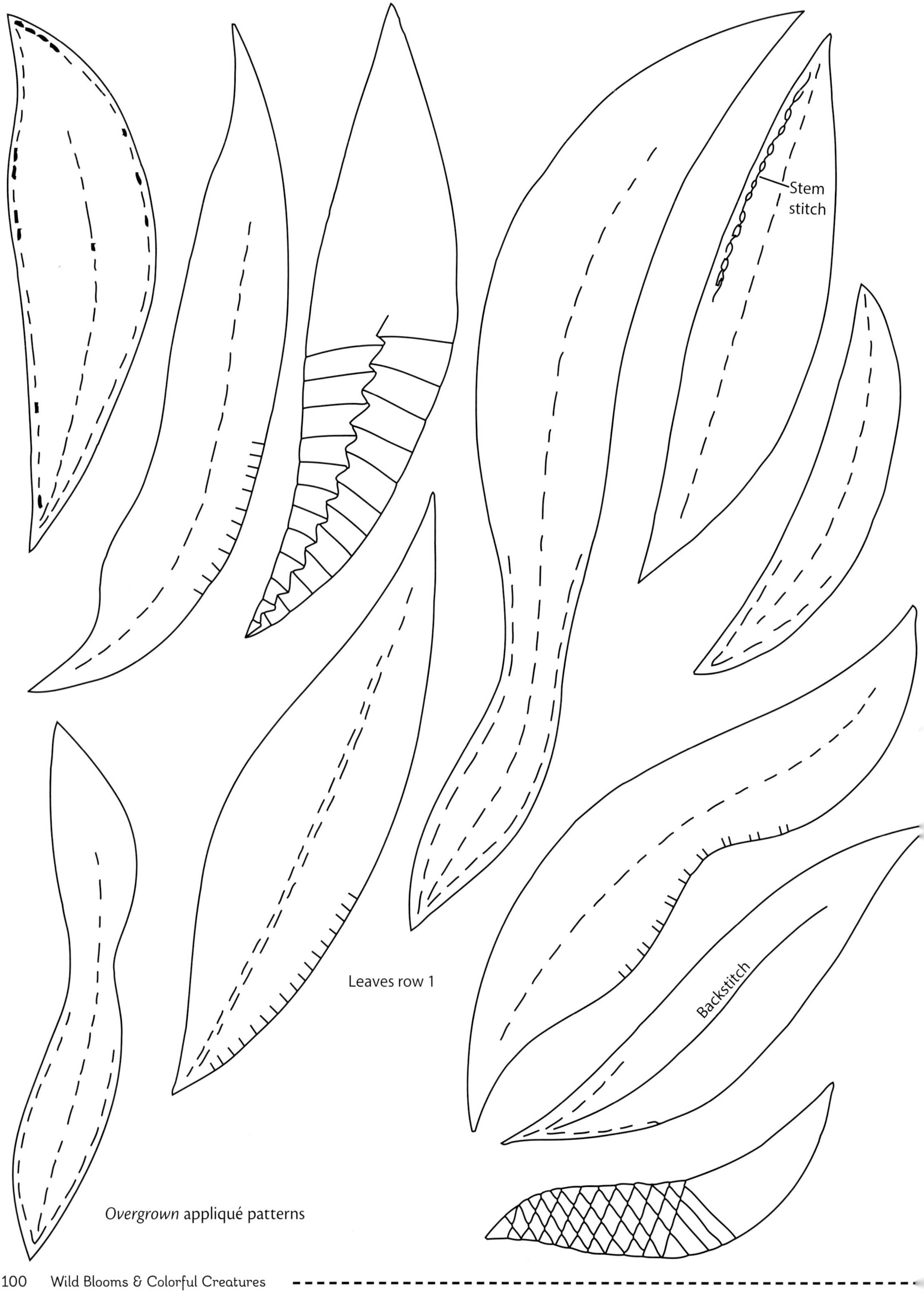

Overgrown appliqué patterns

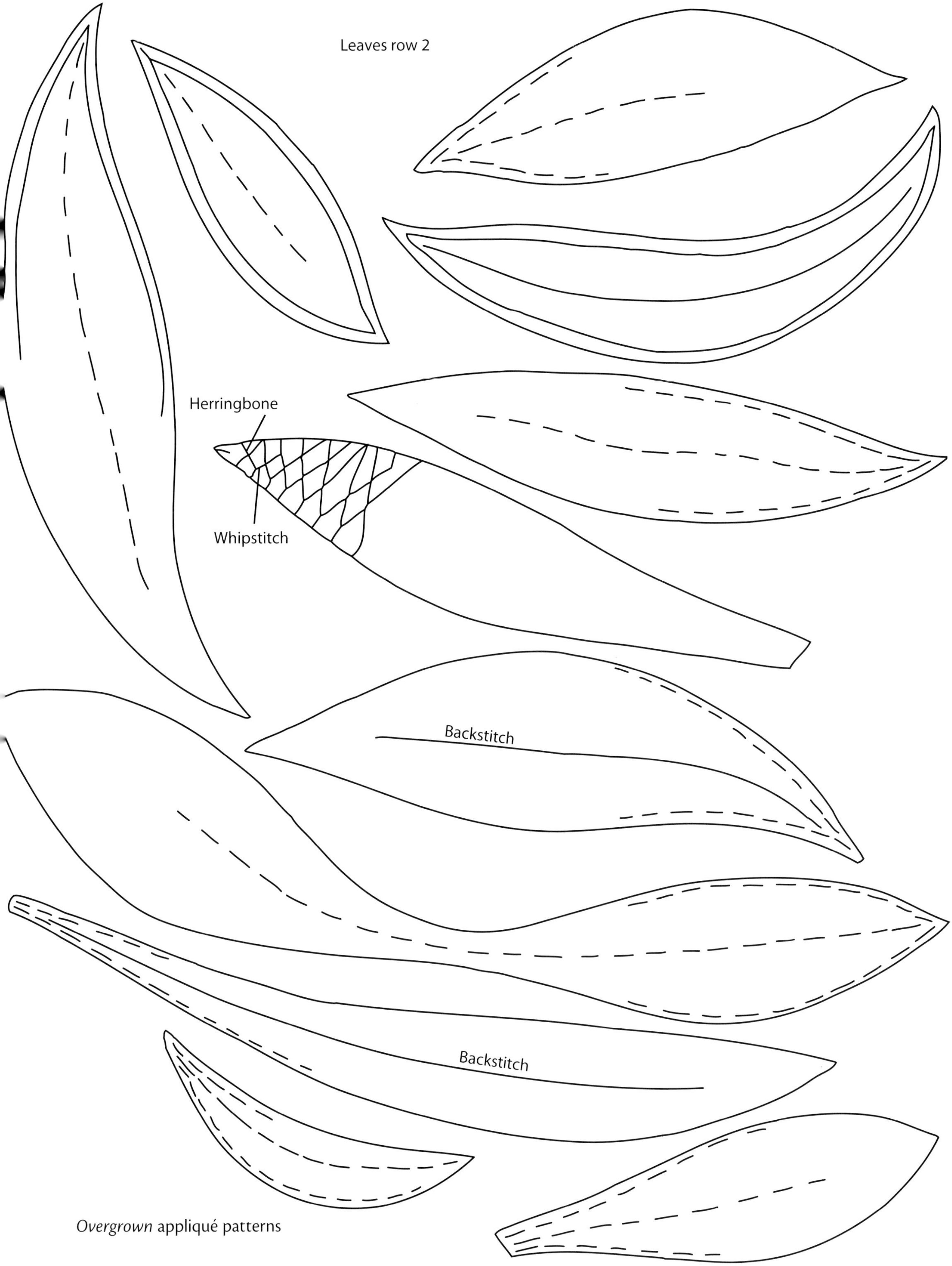

Overgrown appliqué patterns

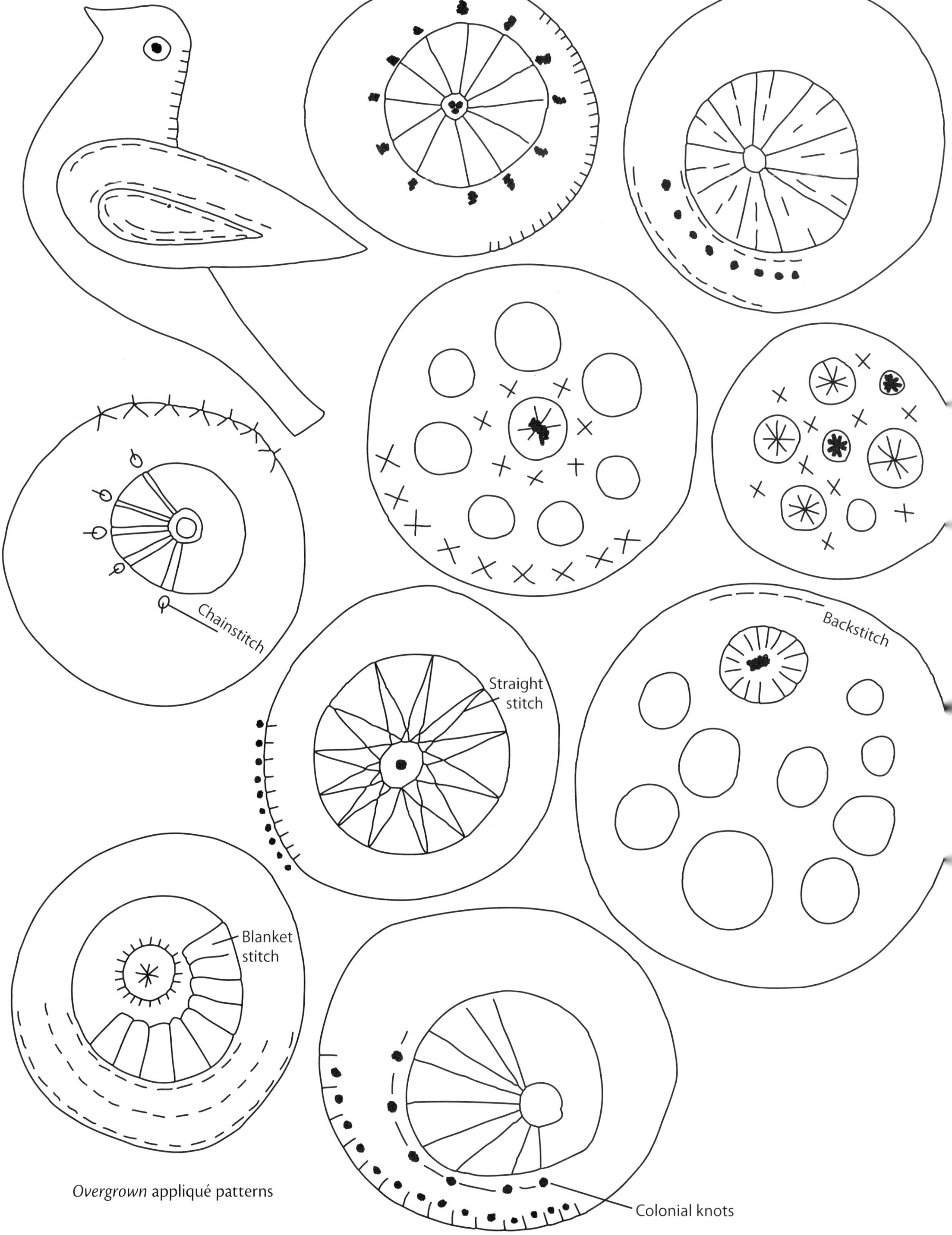

Overgrown appliqué patterns

Overgrown appliqué patterns

Overgrown appliqué patterns

Overgrown appliqué patterns

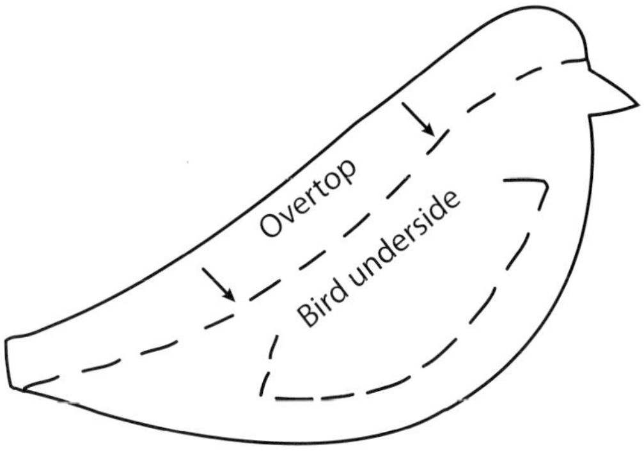

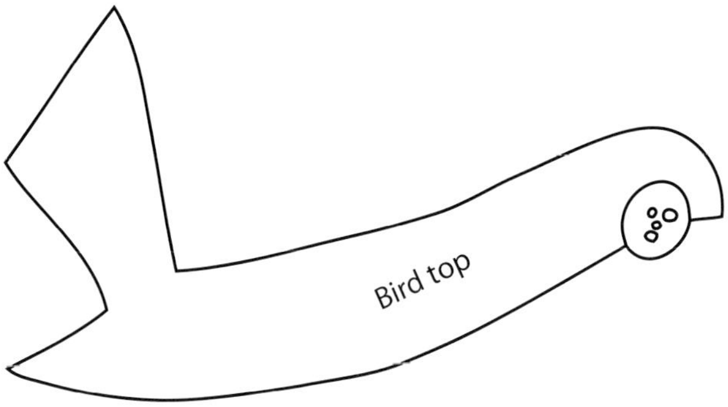

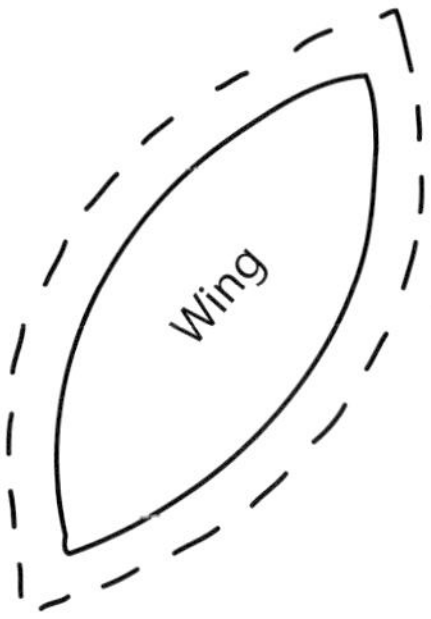

Leaves for flowers

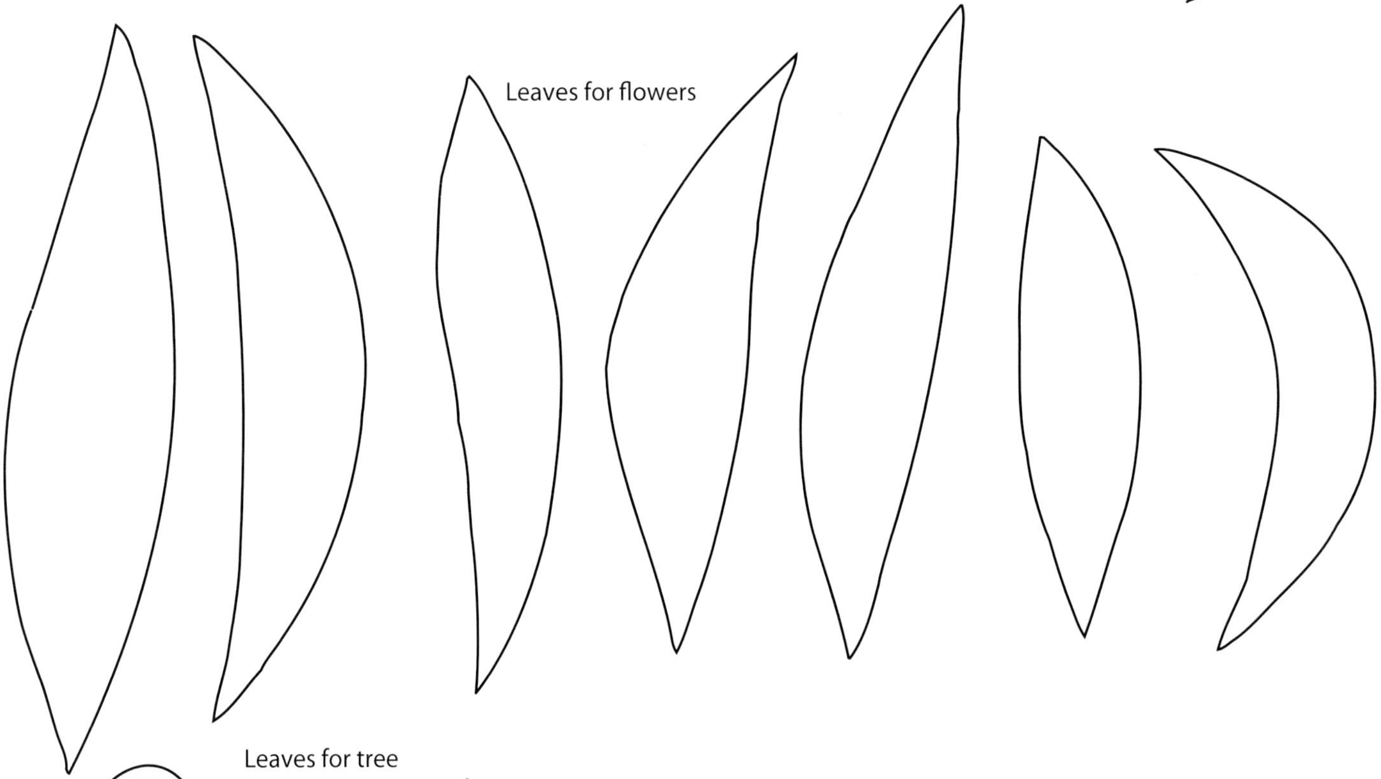

Leaves for tree

Circle centers for tree flowers

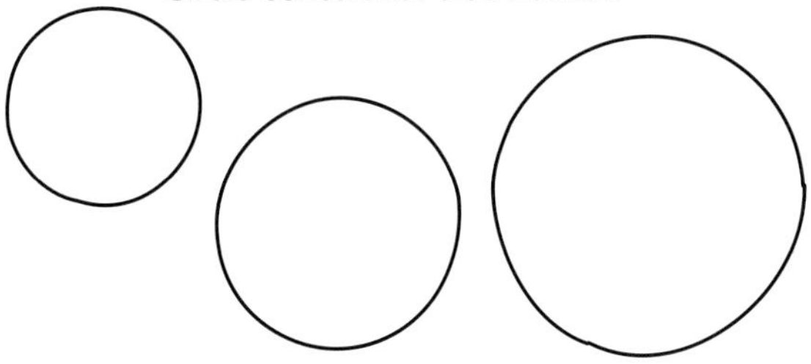

Circle centers for flower garden

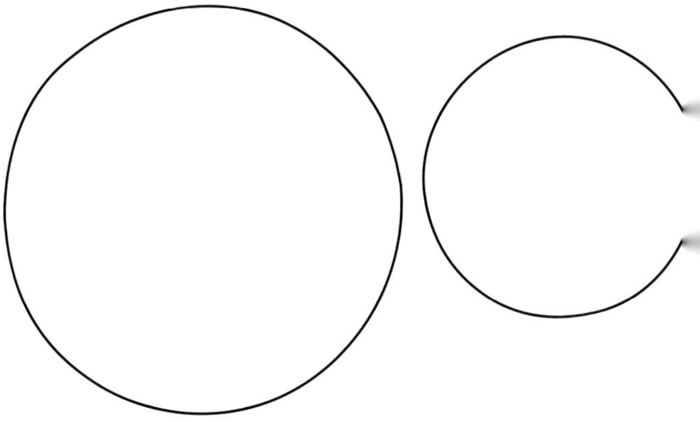

Flowering Tree Runner appliqué patterns

Still Life Pillows
appliqué patterns

Still Life Pillows appliqué patterns

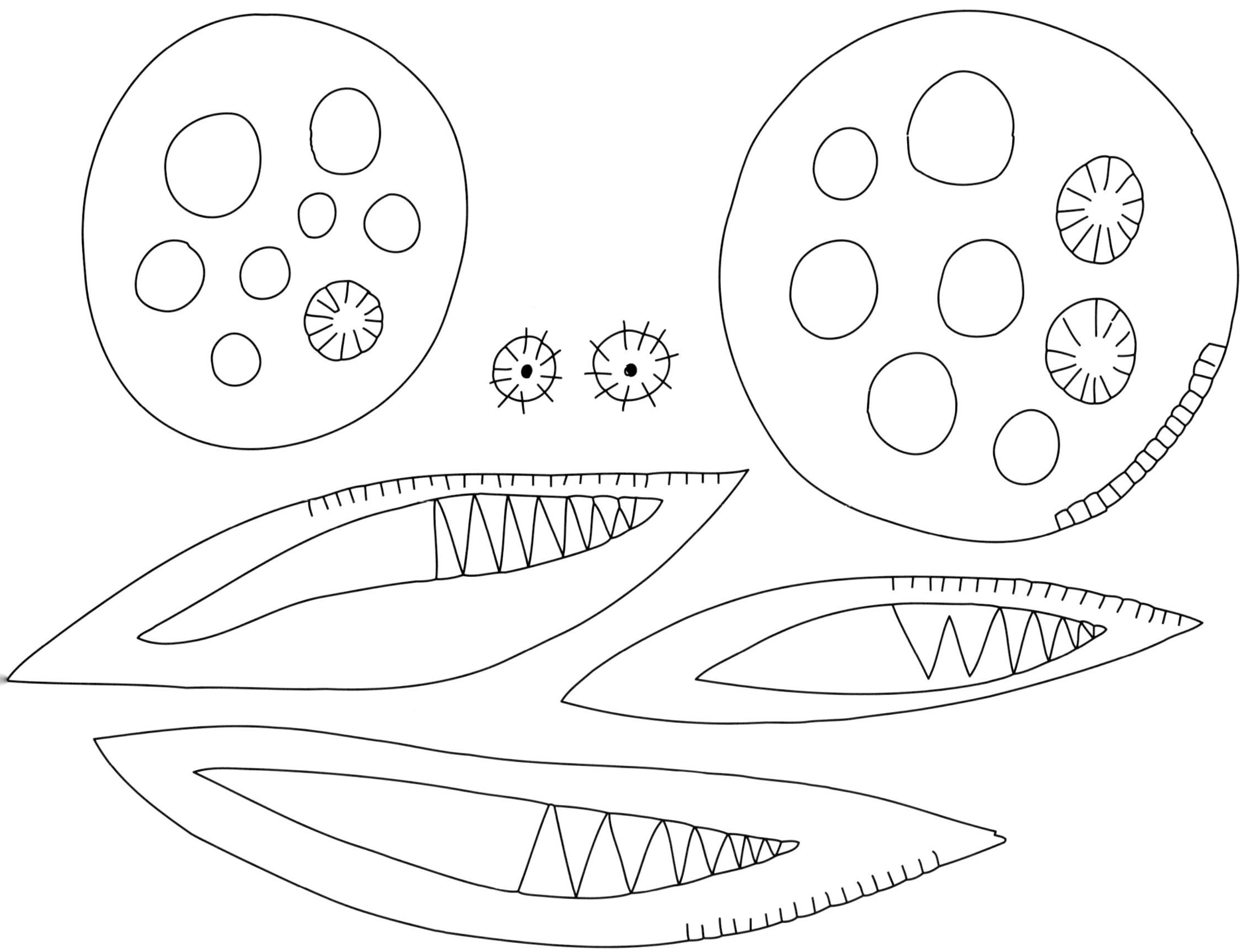

Wildflowers Bag appliqué patterns

Woolly Needle Case appliqué patterns

Little Birds Sewing Kit appliqué patterns

About the Author

Wendy has an extensive background in patchwork and textile design. She studied fashion and teaching after leaving school and went on to work in the fashion industry as a pattern maker / grader and worked as a full-time teacher of fashion.

She started her pattern business, Flying Fish Kits, in 2007 by selling patterns and kits online. Throughout her life, her passion has always been creative needle-work. Her career and her casual life have blended together to create a long series of imaginative designs and ideas. The subjects for these projects are like thought bubbles from her life, and they reflect her house at the beach with underwater themes and her garden at home in Sydney with flowers, trees, and animals.

In 2008, Wendy joined forces with the team at Material Obsession. Since then she has become an invaluable member of the teaching team, while enjoying the colorful fabrics and creative students that frequent her classes. She is a prolific designer with new projects and ideas always on the go in quilts, housewares, clothing, and bags. A mother of two boys and a dog, and happily married to a great cook, Wendy has a life full of accomplishments.

Visit Wendy's website at www.flyingfishkits.com.au.